Risk

...ative care of surgical patients

...Confidential Enquiry into

...ath (2011)

...inator

...les, Cardiff and Vale University

...ICM
...inator
...th NHS Trust

...archer

...al Researcher and Deputy

...ecutive

The authors and trustees of NCEPOD would particularly like to thank the NCEPOD staff for their work in collecting and analysing the data for this study: Robert Alleway, Aysha Butt, Donna Ellis, Heather Freeth, Kathryn Kelly, Dolores Jarman, Sherin Joy, Waqaar Majid, Sabah Mayet, Eva Nwosu and Hannah Shotton.

Special thanks are given to Professor Martin Utley and Professor Steve Gallivan from the Clinical Operational Research Unit at University College London, for their scientific advice.

Designed and published by Dave Terrey
dave.terrey@greysquirrel.co.uk

Contents

Acknowledgements

This report, published by NCEPOD, could not have been achieved without the support of a wide range of individuals who have contributed to this study. Our particular thanks go to:

The Expert Group who advised NCEPOD on what to assess during this study:

Mr Declan Carey	Consultant Upper Gastrointestinal Surgeon (AUGIS)
Professor Gordon Carlson	Consultant General and Intestinal Failure Surgeon (ASGBI)
Ms Deborah Dawson	Consultant Nurse Critical Care
Dr David Goldhill	Consultant and Honorary Reader in Intensive Care Medicine
Professor Michael Gough	Consultant Vascular Surgeon
Mr Alan Horgan	Consultant Colorectal Surgeon
Professor Monty Mythen	Professor of Anaesthesia
Dr Rupert Pearse	Senior Lecturer & Consultant in Intensive Care Medicine
Dr Kathy Rowan	Intensive Care National Audit and Research Centre (ICNARC)
Dr Carl Waldmann	Intensive Care Society

The Advisors who peer reviewed the cases (grade at time of study):

Dr Jeya Anandanesan	Consultant anaesthetist
Dr Peter Berry	Consultant anaesthetist
Dr Poonam Bopanna	ST5 anaesthetist
Dr Mario Calleja	Consultant anaesthetist
Dr Coralie Carle	4th year SpR in anaesthesia and intensive care medicine
Dr Mukesh Chugh	Consultant anaesthetist
Dr Adrian Clarke	ST5 anaesthetist
Mr Michael Corlett	Consultant general surgeon
Ms Jo Coward	Critical care nurse
Ms Karen Dearden	Network service improvement lead
Dr Patrick Dill-Russell	Consultant anaesthetist
Dr Fiona Dodd	Consultant anaesthetist
Dr Richard Elliott	Consultant anaesthetist
Dr Peter Evans	Consultant in anaesthesia and intensive care medicine
Mr Andrew Fordyce	Consultant oral and facial surgeon
Dr Lui Forni	Consultant in intensive care medicine and nephrology
Dr Kirsty Forrest	Consultant anaesthetist
Ms Karin Gerber	Sister, critical care outreach
Mr Richard Gibbs	Consultant vascular surgeon
Ms Sheila Goodman	Sister
Dr Mark Hamilton	Consultant in anaesthesia and intensive care medicine
Mr Chris Hand	Consultant orthopaedic and trauma surgeon
Dr Jeff Handel	Consultant anaesthetist
Mrs Claudia Harding-Mackean	Consultant surgeon
Dr Chris Hingston	Advanced trainee in intensive care medicine

ACKNOWLEDGEMENTS

Dr Rachel Homer	Anaesthetic specialist registrar in anaesthesia and intensive care medicine	Dr Vino Ramachandra	Consultant anaesthetist
Dr Richard Howard-Griffin	Consultant in intensive care medicine	Mr David Ratliff	Consultant surgeon (integrated surgery)
Dr David Hughes	Consultant anaesthetist	Ms Julie Robinson	Senior practice facilitator
Mr Rotimi Jaiyesimi	Consultant obstetrician and gynaecologist	Lt Col Philip Rossell	Consultant trauma and orthopaedic surgeon
Dr Kat James	Consultant anaesthetist	Dr Davina Ross-Anderson	ST6 in anaesthesia
Dr Stephen James	SpR in anaesthesia	Dr Bhaskar Saha	Consultant in intensive care medicine
Dr Diana Jolliffe	Consultant anaesthetist	Ms Amanda Saltmarsh	Matron
Mr Rob Kirby	Consultant surgeon	Dr Martin Schuster-Bruce	Director of critical care
Dr Anton Krige	Consultant in anaesthesia and intensive care medicine	Dr Mahesh Shah	Consultant anaesthetist
Mr Steve Krikler	Consultant trauma and orthopaedic surgeon	Mr Hanif Shiwani	Consultant general surgeon
		Dr V.R. Shylaja	Consultant anaesthetist
Ms Gill Leaver	Sister in intensive care	Dr Kevin Sim	Consultant in critical care medicine
Dr Nicholas Levy	Consultant in anaesthesia, critical care medicine and acute pain	Dr Heather Slowey	Consultant anaesthetist
		Dr Alison Smith	Consultant anaesthetist
Dr Stephen Luney	Consultant neuroanaesthetist	Dr Andrew Smith	Consultant anaesthetist
Dr Sarah Martindale	Consultant anaesthetist	Dr Craig Stenhouse	Consultant in anaesthesia and critical care medicine
Dr Kirstin May	Associate specialist in anaesthesia	Dr Robert Stephens	Consultant anaesthetist
Dr Rina Mehrotra	Consultant anaesthetist	Dr Carole Streets	Final Year SpR in anaesthesia
Mr Anur Miah	Registrar in general surgery	Dr Karen Stuart-Smith	Consultant anaesthetist
Dr Jonathan Mole	Consultant anaesthetist	Dr Sarah Waldron	Specialist Training Year 5 in anaesthesia
Dr Jane Montgomery	Consultant anaesthetist		
Mr Matt Moore	Critical care nurse	Dr Duncan Watson	Consultant in anaesthesia and critical care medicine
Dr Valerie Newman	Consultant anaesthetist	Mr John Welch	Consultant nurse in critical care
Dr David Northwood	Consultant anaesthetist		
Mr Derek O'Reilly	Consultant hepatobiliary and pancreatic surgeon	Dr Sally Wheatley	Consultant anaesthetist
		Dr Maggie Wright	Consultant in critical care medicine
Dr Marlies Ostermann	Consultant nephrologist and critical care physician	Dr Ralph Zumpe	Consultant in anaesthesia and critical care medicine
Dr Umakanth Panchagnula	Consultant in anaesthesia and honorary lecturer		
Dr Ed Pickles	Consultant anaesthetist		
Dr Makani Purva	Consultant anaesthetist		
Dr Kai Rabenstein	Associate specialist in anaesthesia and critical care Medicine		

Foreword

Many of us, when told that peri-operative mortality in the UK is significantly worse than in the USA (see Figure 1) instinctively reach for the null hypothesis. Those who are familiar with healthcare problems in America tell us that their issues are at least as formidable as our own, despite the greater expenditure. However, this report provides a disturbing alternative explanation for the apparently poor results we achieve. The short answer seems to be that people die because we do not give them the level of care they are entitled to expect. The results of this prospective study of all the surgery carried out over one week demonstrate that there is a long way to go in this country before we can suggest that we have reached an acceptable position. In this report less than half of the high-risk patients received care that our advisors thought they would accept from themselves or their own institutions. The reasons for this are straightforward and clearly spelled out.

This report contains cogent evidence that today's patients are more challenging than those the NHS dealt with even ten years ago. Two thirds of them were overweight. A substantial number had significant comorbidities (Figure 3.7). It is to be expected that the patients we study are getting older, like the population they represent: six of these patients were centenarians, the oldest being 104. 184 patients aged 91 or over underwent surgery and I was interested to see that a third of them were regarded as low risk by their anaesthetists (see Figure 3.5).

The difficulty is that the NHS generally does not seem to be rising to the challenge.

The organisational data also demonstrates the gulf between where we are and where we need to be. 18% of hospitals told us that they had no policy for assessing nutritional status and no dietitian was available in 28%

of those that did have a policy (page 21). This cohort of patients underwent their treatment just before NCEPOD published *A Mixed Bag*, our study of parenteral nutrition and this report provides further stark evidence, if it were needed, that nutrition has been an under-appreciated specialty in British hospitals. Only 28 patients in this whole group had a pre-operative plan made to improve their nutrition. Let us hope that this report will reinforce the message of *A Mixed Bag* and that we will see better data in future reports.

The absence of pre-operative planning to improve nutrition pales in significance beside the finding that 16% of the hospitals had no pre-admission anaesthetic assessment clinic, and 17% had no surgical assessment clinic. There were even 5 hospitals that managed without either (Table 2.13). These hospitals really do have to do more to meet the needs of the population that they are now serving and the increasing challenges that lie ahead. It is not right that almost 20% of elective high risk patients were not seen in a pre-assessment clinic. Those who were not had a 30 day mortality almost 7 times as high (4.8% v 0.7%). It is hard to escape the conclusion that those facts are linked.

Our Advisors are in no doubt that we need a UK-wide system that allows rapid and easy identification of patients who are at high risk, and that these people should be recognised as such and managed appropriately. That to me is the most striking take-home message of this Report. Once that is in place we can expect that appropriate planning for a safer journey through the system will follow.

Once patients enter hospital, the organisation still does not improve. Overall, 12% of hospitals had no policy for recognising an acutely ill patient. Again, previous

NCEPOD reports such as *Adding Insult to Injury*, our study of acute kidney injury, demonstrated that many junior doctors and nurses now struggle to identify the patient who is seriously ill. Over a third of hospitals had no policy for preventing peri-operative hypothermia. Despite evidence that haemodynamic monitoring works, only a small minority of high risk cases had arterial lines, central lines or cardiac output monitoring (Table 3.23).

Four hospitals appear to have no post-anaesthetic recovery area at all (Table 2.4), and over 60% of those that did could only provide ventilatory support in an emergency or for a maximum of 6 hours (Figure 2.1). A third of hospitals had no critical care outreach team, which caused our advisors to wonder how they were integrated into the rest of the hospital (page 19). Only 22% of high risk patients went to critical care. The numbers are admittedly small, but the cases where our advisors criticised the decision to send them back to the ward also had a massively increased mortality (5% v 1.4%) (Table 3.5). It seems shocking that 74 high risk non-elective patients went to a ward after surgery and died there with no escalation to critical care (page 42). Of the 165 high risk patients who died, 80 were never admitted to critical care. Our authors speculate that in some cases intra-operative findings may have rendered this appropriate because survival was clearly not possible, but that is unlikely to be a sufficient explanation for many of these cases (page 44).

Society's expectation of the Health Service in areas of communication and safety are increasing all the time. One depressing finding to a lawyer who handles claims against the NHS is the lackadaisical attitude to documenting pre-operative counselling. In the claims I see the consent process is now held up to scrutiny whenever there is a claim in respect of a complication, and the general conclusion is that if it was not written down it did not happen. The documentation of the advice that the patient was given is increasingly seen by judges and the GMC as part of the process by which the doctor demonstrates their respect for the autonomy of the patient.

This report suggests that the NHS still has not caught up and that the distance between what we are achieving and what we aspire to achieve is showing no signs of getting narrower. Amongst 496 high risk patients, the consenting patient seems to have been given an estimate of mortality in only 37 (7.5%) cases according to the notes. These doctors are still applying the standards of benevolent paternalism that society and the GMC expected in the 1970s. Our society increasingly expects patients to be managed with Decision Aids and other professional techniques for raising the quality of the patient's understanding of what is involved and their participation in decisions about their treatment.

As always, we are grateful to our experts, advisors and authors who do so much to make these reports happen. Their commitment demonstrates how much determination there is to improve the delivery of health care.

Mr Bertie Leigh, Chair of NCEPOD

Principal Recommendations

There is a need to introduce a UK wide system that allows rapid and easy identification of patients who are at high risk of postoperative mortality and morbidity. (Departments of Health in England, Wales & Northern Ireland)

All elective high risk patients should be seen and fully investigated in pre-assessment clinics. Arrangements should be in place to ensure more urgent surgical patients have the same robust work up. (Clinical Directors and Consultants)

An assessment of mortality risk should be made explicit to the patient and recorded clearly on the consent form and in the medical record. (Consultants)

The postoperative care of the high risk surgical patient needs to be improved. Each Trust must make provision for sufficient critical care beds or pathways of care to provide appropriate support in the postoperative period. (Medical Directors)

To aid planning for provision of facilities for high risk patients, each Trust should analyse the volume of work considered to be high risk and quantify the critical care requirements of this cohort. This assessment and plan should be reported to the Trust Board on an annual basis. (Medical Directors)

Introduction

Advances in surgical and patient care continue to deliver overall good patient outcomes despite an aging population, increasing comorbidities and ever expanding surgical therapies. Risk of death and major complications after surgery in the general surgical patient population are low: less than 1% of all patients undergoing surgery die during the same hospital admission[1].

Despite this overall low death rate, mortality in some groups of patients can be surprisingly high. It is estimated that around 20000 - 25000 deaths per year occur in hospital after a surgical procedure, across the UK. Of these deaths approximately 80% occur in a small population of patients. This population is known by the term 'high risk patients'. High risk patients are estimated to make up approximately 10% of the overall inpatient surgical workload and are a major source of not only mortality but also morbidity and resource utilisation. This population of high risk patients has a hospital mortality rate of approximately 10-15%[2].

There are concerns that UK outcomes may be less good than outcomes in other countries. It appears that the NHS as a whole has poorer outcomes compared with centres in similar sized hospitals and patient populations in the United States of America (USA)[3,4].

The data below show that UK mortality appears to be noticeably greater than US mortality – eight fold in the predicted risk of death group 0-5% to three fold in the predicted risk of death group 11-20%.

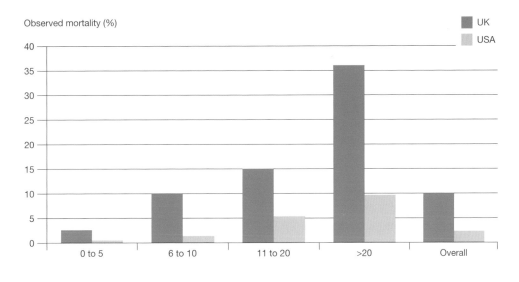

Figure 1. Observed deaths for case-mix adjusted patients undergoing major, non-cardiac surgery in UK and USA cohorts over the same time period and in comparable hospitals.[3]

There are several steps to addressing this problem.

1. Identification of the high risk group

The first challenge is to reliably and accurately identify the patient group that is at high risk of mortality and morbidity. Whilst this might seem obvious, the literature is full of differing descriptions, scoring systems and tests to meet this aim. They are largely based on assessment of comorbidities alone or combined with a classification of surgical intervention. Tests of organ function and more recently of physiological reserve are also used to try to address this issue.

2. Improved pre-operative assessment, triage and preparation

Measures to improve fitness for surgery can be targeted and applied if the identification of these high risk patients can be performed in a suitable timescale. Usually this process is thought of as having started once the patient has been accepted for surgery but more recent developments identify primary care as a key partner in identifying fitness for surgery. As well as specific optimisation of comorbidities it is important to manage volaemic status and nutritional status. Recently there has been interest in improving physiological reserve, using exercise regimens, where appropriate. There is also the opportunity to consider if surgical intervention is the best course of action due to the risk of adverse outcomes.

3. Improved intra-operative care

Once this high risk patient group can be reliably identified the next challenge, if a surgical pathway is the proposed treatment, is to improve the process of care. This will potentially improve survival, reduce morbidity and as a consequence potentially consume less health care resources. There is substantial evidence to help us meet these aims for our patients. Use of cardiac output monitoring and fluid optimisation has been studied in many groups of patients including colorectal, trauma and vascular patients. Most results support the use of peri-operative optimisation in high risk patients undergoing major surgery. Pre-optimisation before and during surgery[5-10] in a protocolised manner improves patient outcomes in high risk surgical patients. Meta-analysis, including all available studies, confirms an improvement in mortality[11]. More recent work has confirmed that these benefits are realisable in everyday practice[12]. In addition, the National Institute for Health and Clinical Excellence (NICE) has issued guidance to support this area[13].

4. Improved use of postoperative resources

In many other countries, patients undergoing major surgery routinely receive a higher level of postoperative care than is delivered in the UK to NHS patients. In part this may be due to resources allocated to critical care. The proportion of hospital beds allocated to critical care in the UK is lower than comparable countries. In addition the UK has a pattern of critical care beds that may not be maximally efficient, with high numbers of units operating with fewer than six beds. The challenge faced is to ensure that patients receive the level of postoperative care they require to achieve optimal outcomes, recognising that a vast increase in critical care beds is not likely.

It can be seen that there are significant challenges regarding the identification and care pathway of high risk surgical patients. However, much of the data are pieced together from institutional studies and extrapolated or gained from databases for which the initial purpose was not to study this group. Whereas the study described in this report was undertaken specifically to provide an overview of current care for all surgical patients with a particular focus on the high risk group and to provide a baseline assessment of the current status of care, what remediable factors are evident and what needs to be done to improve the care of such patients.

1 – Method and Data Returns

Study aim

To carry out a national review of the peri-operative care of patients undergoing inpatient surgery.

Expert group

An Expert Group was formed to steer this study and determine the objectives of the work. This comprised a multidisciplinary group of consultants from intensive care medicine, anaesthesia, surgery (including upper gastrointestinal, vascular and colorectal), critical care nursing, a representative from ICNARC, and scientific Advisors, who all contributed to the design of the study, and reviewed the findings.

Objectives

The Expert Group identified six main objectives that would address the primary aim of the study, and these will be addressed throughout the following chapters:

- Patient factors
- Pre-operative assessment
- Anaesthetic factors
- Surgical factors
- Postoperative care
- Complications

Hospital participation

National Health Service hospitals in England, Wales and Northern Ireland were expected to participate, as well as hospitals in the independent sector and public hospitals in the Isle of Man, Guernsey and Jersey.

Within each hospital, a named contact, referred to as the NCEPOD Local Reporter, acted as a link between NCEPOD and the hospital staff, facilitating dissemination of questionnaires and data collation.

Study population

All patients aged 16 or over were eligible for inclusion in the prospective element of the study if they underwent specific inpatient surgery between 1st and 7th March 2010 inclusive.

To be included in the peer review aspect of the study the patients had to have been described as high risk by the anaesthetist completing the prospective form.

Exclusions

Patients were excluded from the study if they had day surgery with no planned overnight stay, or were obstetric, cardiac, transplant or neurosurgery cases.

Method

All patients who underwent inpatient surgery, both elective and emergency, during the study period and met the study criteria, were included. Data collection took place in two stages. Firstly, prospective data were collected at the time the patient was operated on, to allow prompt identification of patients undergoing surgery during the defined sample week. The second stage of data collection used the standard NCEPOD method of case review by asking NCEPOD Local Reporters to identify all patients retrospectively who underwent surgery in the same given time period via the hospital patient administration systems. This was to allow cross checking to ensure the captured prospective sample was representative and to allow identification of the consultant at the time of discharge and the outcome of the patient. From this data a group of patients, defined as high risk, were randomly selected for detailed peer review.

Organisational questionnaire

To assess the facilities available at each site performing surgery an organisational questionnaire was sent to the NCEPOD Local Reporter for completion in collaboration with relevant specialty input. A letter outlining the request was also sent to the Medical Director. The information requested in this questionnaire included information on operating facilities, theatre availability, special care areas, and pre-operative assessment facilities.

Definition of risk

As the purpose of this study was to examine the care of high risk patients it is important to describe how patients were classified as high risk or low risk. The stratification of risk could have been based on patient comorbidities, age, urgency of surgery and procedure performed. However, for the purpose of this study we asked the anaesthetist, who filled out the prospective data collection form, whether they considered the patient to be high risk. No definition of what constituted a high risk patient was provided and this classification was therefore shaped by the anaesthetists' knowledge of the high risk surgical literature and their own perception of risk in the context of their own institution. This pragmatic definition was used for several reasons:

1. Classification of risk was determined prospectively, with no knowledge of outcome.
2. Where patients were classified as high risk it is reasonable to expect that processes would be in place to treat the patient according to the perception of risk, as this was decided by the treating physician within their own organisation.
3. Clinician stratification of risk could be compared during analysis to established systems using factors such as patient comorbidities, age, urgency of surgery and procedure performed to determine agreement.

Patients who were not classified as high risk will be referred to as low risk in this report to allow the two groups to be easily differentiated.

Chapter 4 will address the use of standardised risk scoring systems, and compare the data with that collected in the pragmatic approach adopted by this study. There are many such risk scoring systems, and the Revised Cardiac Risk Index of Lee et al[14] for stratifying risk before noncardiac surgery has been selected to use as an example of how such systems work. This validated index consists of six independent predictors of complications:

- High-risk surgery (intraperitoneal, intrathoracic, or suprainguinal vascular procedures)
- Ischaemic heart disease
- History of congestive heart failure
- History of cerebrovascular disease
- Insulin therapy for diabetes mellitus
- Pre-operative creatinine level greater than 176 micromol/l.

The more predictors a patient has, the greater the risk of peri-operative complications. Each predictor adds one point to the final score and is associated with a Lee class and risk of major cardiac complications (myocardial infarction, pulmonary oedema, complete heart block, cardiac arrest).

Table 1.1 Lee class and risk

Points	Class	Risk
0	I	0.4%
1	II	0.9%
2	III	6.6%
3 or more	IV	11%

Case ascertainment – prospective data

Patients undergoing inpatient surgery were identified by anaesthetists who completed a clinical form prospectively at the time of surgery. The information requested included ASA class, comorbidities, urgency of surgery, postoperative location (preferred and actual), and whether they considered the patient to be a high risk patient. If the patient went to a recovery room, a small section of the form was also completed by the recovery room staff. This method ensured that data were collected accurately with regard to patient location and movements at the time of surgery, details that are often not clear from the case notes and hard to obtain retrospectively.

Case ascertainment – retrospective case data

Local reporters retrospectively used patient identifiers from the forms to link to 30 day outcome data including identifying patients who were admitted to level 2 or 3 critical care. These data were sent to NCEPOD on password protected spreadsheets and imported to a secure database.

Case ascertainment – peer review data

From those patients who had both a clinical form and outcome data, up to six high risk patients per hospital were selected at random by NCEPOD and included in the case note review by Advisors.

Photocopied case note extracts were requested for each case that was to be peer reviewed which included:
- Inpatient annotations, including the pre-operative assessment, admission clerking notes and notes for the first consultant ward round
- Nursing notes
- Level 2/Level 3 notes
- Nutrition notes
- Anaesthetic record
- Any operating notes
- Biochemistry results
- Haematology results
- Drug charts (including parenteral nutrition prescription chart)
- Fluid balance charts
- Observation charts
- Discharge summary
- Post mortem report, if applicable

These were anonymised upon receipt at NCEPOD.

Advisor group

A multidisciplinary group of Advisors was recruited to review the case notes and associated clinical form of each patient selected. The group of Advisors comprised consultants, associate specialists, nurses and trainees, from the following specialties: anaesthesia, intensive care medicine, critical care and surgery.

Clinical forms and case notes were anonymised by the non-clinical staff at NCEPOD. All patient, clinician and hospital identifiers were removed. Neither Clinical Co-ordinators at NCEPOD, nor the Advisors, had access to identifiable information.

After being anonymised, each case was reviewed by one Advisor within a multidisciplinary group. At regular intervals throughout the meeting, the Chair allowed a period of discussion for each Advisor to summarise their case and ask for opinions from other specialties or raise aspects of the case for discussion.

The grading system below was used by the Advisors to grade the overall care each patient received:

Good practice: A standard that you would accept from yourself, your trainees and your institution.
Room for improvement: Aspects of **clinical** care that could have been better.
Room for improvement: Aspects of **organisational** care that could have been better.
Room for improvement: Aspects of both **clinical and organisational** care that could have been better.
Less than satisfactory: Several aspects of clinical and/or organisational care that were well below that you would accept from yourself, your trainees and your institution.
Insufficient data: Insufficient information submitted to NCEPOD to assess the quality of care.

Quality and confidentiality

Each case was given a unique NCEPOD number so that cases could not be easily linked to a hospital.

The data from all questionnaires received were electronically scanned into a preset database. Prior to any analysis taking place, the data were cleaned to ensure that there were no duplicate records and that erroneous data had not been entered during scanning. Any fields that contained spurious data that could not be validated were removed.

Data analysis

Following cleaning of the quantitative data, descriptive data summaries were produced and the qualitative data collected from the Advisors' opinions were coded, where applicable, according to content to allow quantitative analysis. The data were reviewed by NCEPOD Clinical Co-ordinators, a Researcher, and a Clinical Researcher, to identify the nature and frequency of recurring themes.

Case studies

Case studies have been used through the peer review section of this report to illustrate particular themes.

All data were analysed using Microsoft Access and Excel by the research staff at NCEPOD and the findings of the report were reviewed by the Expert Group, Advisors and the NCEPOD Steering Group prior to publication.

Data returns

Organisational questionnaire
There were 301 questionnaires returned.

Prospective forms and case notes for review

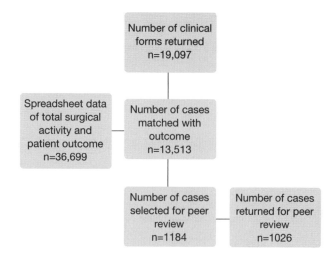

Figure 1.2 Data returned

19,097 clinical forms were included in the analysis of prospective data and a sample were also used by the Advisors during the peer review. In total, 829 cases were assessed by the Advisors. The remainder of the returned case note extracts were either too incomplete for assessment or were returned after the final deadline and last Advisor meeting.

Study sample denominator by chapter

Within this study the denominator will change for each chapter and occasionally within each chapter. This is because data have been taken from different sources depending on the analysis required. For example in some cases the data presented will be a total from a question taken from the prospective form only, whereas some analysis may have required the prospective form and the Advisors' view taken from the case notes.

2 – Organisational Data

Before reviewing the prospective and peer review data this chapter aims to provide an overview of the availability of certain key facilities, policies and clinical pathways that would be relevant to the care of surgical, and in particular high risk surgical patients. All hospital sites undertaking inpatient surgery were asked to complete an organisational questionnaire.

Theatre availability

Tables 2.1-2.3 show availability of a theatre staffed to deal with emergency/urgent surgery (CEPOD theatre) during Monday – Friday. Independent hospitals have been excluded from these tables.

Table 2.1 Emergency theatres – day time

Emergency theatre 08.00 - 17.59	Number of hospitals	%
Yes	158	72.5
No	60	27.5
Subtotal	218	
Not answered	9	
Total	227	

Table 2.2 Emergency theatres – evening

Emergency theatre 18.00 - 23.59	Number of hospitals	%
Yes	183	83.2
No	37	16.8
Subtotal	220	
Not answered	7	
Total	227	

Table 2.3 Emergency theatres – night time

Emergency theatre 00.00 - 07.59	Number of hospitals	%
Yes	183	83.2
No	37	16.8
Subtotal	220	
Not answered	7	
Total	227	

Resources have been concentrated on elective patients for many years and the lack of access for emergency/urgent patients has been a focus of previous NCEPOD reports. Daytime, staffed and available operating theatres (CEPOD theatres) have increased in availability over the years[15-17] and it is encouraging to see that provision of this important facility continues to be high. However, given the growth in emergency/urgent cases there are concerns that patients may still face substantial delays in getting to theatre. Good prioritisation of cases and effective use of this resource is essential.

Availability of a post anaesthetic recovery area

The availability of a post anaesthetic recovery area is shown in Table 2.4.

Of the 293 hospitals from which an answer to this question was received 289 stated that they had this facility. Of the 289 hospitals with a recovery area, 192 were reported as being available 24 hours a day and 7 days per week (Table 2.5).

Table 2.6 shows that 203/262 hospitals stated it was possible to provide ventilatory support and ongoing management in the recovery area.

Table 2.4 Post anaesthetic recovery area

Post anaesthetic recovery area	Number of hospitals	%
Yes	289	98.6
No	4	1.4
Subtotal	293	
Not answered	8	
Total	301	

Table 2.5 Post anaesthetic recovery area, all day every day

Post anaesthetic recovery area all day, every day	Number of hospitals	%
Yes	192	66.9
No	95	33.1
Subtotal	287	
Not answered	2	
Total	289	

Table 2.6 Ventilatory support

Ventilatory support and ongoing management	Number of hospitals	%
Yes	203	77.5
No	59	22.5
Subtotal	262	
Not answered	27	
Total	289	

Table 2.7 Ventilatory support in post anaesthetic recovery areas staffed all day every day

Ventilatory support and ongoing management	Number of hospitals	%
Yes	159	82.8
No	33	17.2
Total	**192**	

Table 2.7 shows these data for recovery units that are staffed and available 24 hours a day, 7 days per week.

Even in recovery areas that were staffed and available 24 hours a day, 7 days per week 17% could not provide this level of support under certain conditions (Table 2.7).

Figure 2.1 Scope of the recovery room in respect of providing ventilatory support and ongoing management.

These data are for all hospitals where a response indicated that ventilatory support and ongoing management (203/262) could be provided. Over 60% of recovery units could only provide this level of support in an emergency or on a short term (defined as up to 6 hours) basis (Figure 2.1).

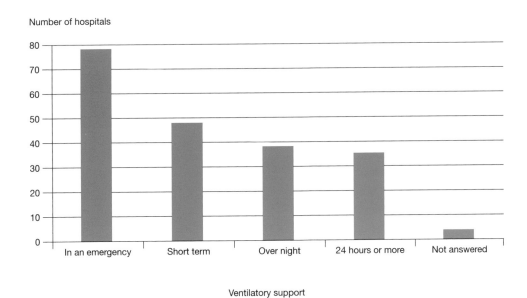

Number of hospitals

Ventilatory support

Figure 2.1 Scope of the recovery room in respect of providing ventilatory support and ongoing management

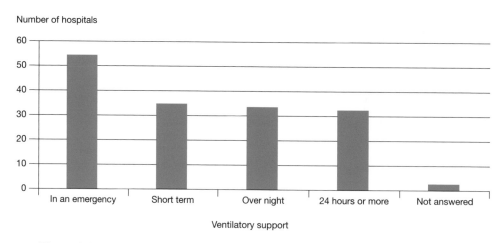

Number of hospitals

Figure 2.2 Provision of ventilatory support in units available all day, every day

Figure 2.2 shows the data for recovery units that were staffed and available 24 hours a day, 7 days per week and that could provide ventilatory support and ongoing management (161/194 hospitals).

Even in hospitals that had continuously staffed and available recovery areas, the majority (57%) could only provide immediate or short term (defined as up to 6 hours) ventilatory support and ongoing management.

Critical care unit provision and systems for the recognition of the critically ill patient

The provision of a critical care unit is shown in Table 2.8

NICE Clinical Guideline 50 (NICE CG 50)[18] describes the requirements for each hospital to have a system to recognise and initiate appropriate management of acutely unwell patients. Table 2.9 shows these data.

It is of particular note that 27/232 hospitals (12%), from which a response was received, did not have a policy for the recognition and management of acutely ill patients (Table 2.9). Many reports have highlighted delayed recognition and delayed initiation of appropriate therapy as a major patient safety problem[19] and this level of non-compliance with NICE guidance is of concern.

Table 2.8 Provision of a critical care unit

Critical care unit	Number of hospitals	%
Yes	236	79.5
No	61	20.5
Subtotal	**297**	
Not answered	4	
Total	**301**	

Table 2.9 System to recognise critically ill patients

Formal policy in line with Clinical Guideline 50 (NICE)	Number of hospitals	%
Yes	205	88.4
No	27	11.6
Subtotal	**232**	
Not answered	69	
Total	**301**	

Table 2.10 Policy for recognising acutely ill patients if the hospital had a critical care unit

Formal policy in line with Clinical Guideline 50 (NICE)	Number of hospitals	%
Yes	184	90.2
No	20	9.8
Subtotal	204	
Not answered	32	
Total	236	

Table 2.10 shows the same analysis, but for hospitals in which it was stated that a critical care unit was available (236 hospitals).

It is to be expected that hospitals that have resourced a critical care unit have done so with due regard to the case mix and need of the hospital population and that the likelihood of patients being acutely unwell would be greater. It is therefore noteworthy that 20/204 hospitals from which a response was received, did not have a policy for recognising and managing acutely ill patients.

Critical care outreach service

One element of recognising and managing acute illness is the provision of a critical care outreach team. These teams, who have a variety of names, function as a link between critical care and wards, provide education on recognition and initial management of acute illness, support patient care and facilitate management of acutely ill patients (either by providing the support necessary to allow the patient to be cared for in the ward environment or by facilitating early admission to critical care).

Over one third of hospitals did not have a critical care outreach team. The non-response rate was 16% (Table 2.11).

The availability of a critical care outreach team for those hospitals where it was indicated that they did have a critical care unit is shown in Table 2.12.

Of those hospitals with a critical care unit 27% responded that they did not have a critical care outreach team and this raises questions of how the critical care unit interfaces effectively with the rest of the hospital.

Table 2.11 Availability of critical care outreach teams

Outreach team	Number of hospitals	%
Yes	166	65.6
No	87	34.4
Subtotal	253	
Not answered	48	
Total	301	

Table 2.12 Critical care outreach team in those hospitals with a critical care unit

Outreach team	Number of hospitals	%
Yes	164	73.5
No	59	26.5
Subtotal	223	
Not answered	13	
Total	236	

Table 2.13 Anaesthetic and surgical pre-admission clinics

Pre-admission anaesthetic clinics	Pre-admission surgical clinics				
	Yes	No	Subtotal	Not answered	Total
Yes	196	43	239	8	247
No	39	5	44	1	45
Subtotal	235	48	283	9	292
Not answered	2	0	2	7	9
Total	237	48	285	16	301

Table 2.14 Policy for assessing nutritional status

Policies for assessing nutritional status	Number of hospitals	%
Yes	238	81.8
No	53	18.2
Subtotal	291	
Not answered	10	
Total	301	

Pre-operative assessment

The facility to assess patients' fitness for surgery is a key aspect in providing optimal care. This should happen early so that remediable factors can be identified and managed, the best treatment plan agreed and the facilities needed to support that treatment plan identified. Table 2.13 shows data on the provision of both anaesthetic and surgical pre-admission assessment clinics.

239/283 hospitals provided pre-admission anaesthetic assessment clinics (84%). 235/283 hospitals provided surgical pre-admission assessment clinics (83%). Of note 5/283 hospitals did not provide either type of pre-admission assessment clinic.

Table 2.15 Dietitian included in the nutrition policy

Does the policy include dietitian involvement	Number of hospitals	%
Yes	164	72.2
No	63	27.8
Subtotal	227	
Not answered	11	
Total	238	

Nutritional status

Pre-operative nutritional state has a predictive value for both morbidity and mortality after major surgery. If recognised early then there is the opportunity to intervene and improve nutritional status. There are widely available tools to help recognise this treatable and potentially reversible comorbidity[20].

Almost one in five hospitals did not have a policy for assessing nutritional status (Table 2.14).

Where hospitals did have policies in place for assessing nutritional status, we asked if this policy included the involvement of a dietician. As can be seen in Table 2.15, the policy included the involvement of a dietitian in less than three quarters of hospitals. This was surprising as patients who are assessed as high risk of nutritional impairment should be referred to a dietitian for expert advice and support.

Cardiopulmonary exercise testing

Cardiopulmonary exercise (CPEX) testing provides objective information on physiological reserve and can be used to risk stratify patients pre-operatively.

Table 2.16 shows that 60% of hospitals responding to this question did not have the facility to undertake CPEX testing on their patients.

Table 2.16 Availability of CPEX testing

Facility for CPEX testing	Number of hospitals	%
Yes	117	40.2
No	174	59.8
Subtotal	291	
Not answered	10	
Total	301	

Available policies for the care of the surgical patient

Much of the organisational data relied on the questioning about existence of policies. It is very difficult to obtain reliable data on implementation of policy but where it can be identified that policies do not exist then this raises questions about how robust processes of care can be in those organisations. This is particularly so where NICE[21] or other national guidance exists.

Table 2.17 Protocol for prophylaxis of venous thromboembolism

Protocol for prophylaxis of venous thromboembolism	Number of hospitals	%
Yes	293	99.3
No	2	0.7
Subtotal	295	
Not answered	6	
Total	301	

Table 2.18 Cross directorate policy on avoidance of peri-operative hypothermia

Cross directorate policy on avoidance of peri-operative hypothermia	Number of hospitals	%
Yes	191	66.3
No	97	33.7
Subtotal	288	
Not answered	13	
Total	301	

Table 2.19 Protocol for peri-operative management of diabetes mellitus

Protocol for peri-operative management of diabetes mellitus	Number of hospitals	%
Yes	259	88.1
No	35	11.9
Subtotal	**294**	
Not answered	7	
Total	**301**	

The availability of policies or protocols for prophylaxis of venous thrombosis, avoidance of peri-operative hypothermia and management of peri-operative diabetes mellitus are shown in Tables 2.17-2.19.

Whilst it appears that protocols for prophylaxis of venous thrombosis are almost uniformly in place (Table 2.17) it was disappointing to see the high number of hospitals without a policy to avoid hypothermia (Table 2.18). This is particularly so given the NICE guidance[21] in this area and the knowledge that hypothermia is associated with morbidity and can be avoided.

Key Findings – Organisational data

158/218 (72.5%) of NHS hospitals had availability of dedicated emergency theatres 08.00-17.59 during Monday to Friday.

289/293 hospitals had a post anaesthetic recovery area. Of these hospitals only 192 sites (67%) have twenty four hours per day, seven days per week provision.

203 hospitals responding stated that they could provide ventilatory support and ongoing management in the post anaesthetic recovery area. 59 hospitals (23%) could not provide this level of support.

Most hospitals (127/200 – 64%) could only provide ventilatory support and ongoing management in the post anaesthetic recovery room for short periods (up to 6 hours).

27/232 hospitals (12%) did not have a formal policy in line with NICE Clinical Guideline 50 for the recognition and initial response to acutely unwell patients.

87/253 hospitals (34%) did not have a critical care outreach team.

44/283 hospitals (16%) did not provide pre-admission anaesthetic assessment clinics.

48/283 hospitals (17%) did not provide pre-admission surgical assessment clinics.

Only 117/291 hospitals (40%) had the facility to undertake cardiopulmonary exercise testing on their patients.

97/288 hospitals (34%) did not have a policy for the prevention of peri-operative hypothermia.

3 – Prospective Data

The data presented in this chapter covers the prospective data that were collected on all eligible surgical patients during the study period. This is the first time that NCEPOD has collected such prospective data. This method was chosen as it was believed that denominator data was important to fully understand the pattern of peri-operative care for all surgical patients.

This section provides an overview of the total sample. As the chapter progresses some of these analyses will be repeated to assess specific areas against risk and against outcome at 30 days post operation (and sometimes both).

3.1 Total population data

Basic demographics are given in Figures 3.1-3.4 and Table 3.1.

The age range was 16-104 years, (mean of 56 years, standard deviation of 19). 55% of the population was female.

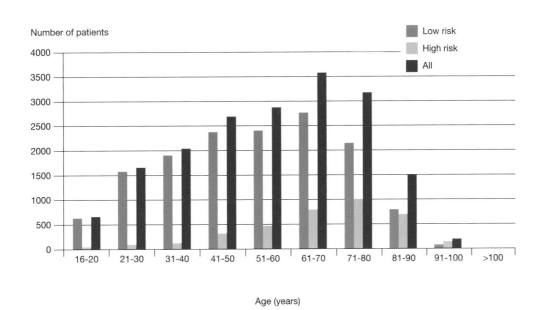

Figure 3.1 Age in years of the prospective study population

Table 3.1 BMI of all patients

BMI	Number of patients	%
<16.5	71	0.4
16.5 – 18.49	238	1.4
18.5 – 24.99	5313	32.0
25 – 29.99	6013	36.2
30 – 34.99	2977	17.9
35 – 39.99	1195	7.2
≥ 40	807	4.9
Subtotal	**16614**	
Could not calculate	2483	
Total	**19097**	

Table 3.2 Classification of BMI

Classification	BMI
Severely underweight	< 16.5
Underweight	16.5 – 18.49
Normal	18.5 – 24.99
Overweight	25 – 29.99
Obese class I	30 – 34.99
Obese class II	35 – 39.99
Obese class III	≥ 40

Only 1 in 3 patients were within a normal BMI range. Two thirds of patients were overweight and of this group over 40% were obese.

Height and weight was provided for 16614 patients and allowed calculation of Body Mass Index (BMI). Table 3.2 provides the classification of weight based on BMI ranges.

The ASA grade of the total population is shown in Figure 3.2. Nearly 80% of the total population was considered to be ASA 1 or 2.

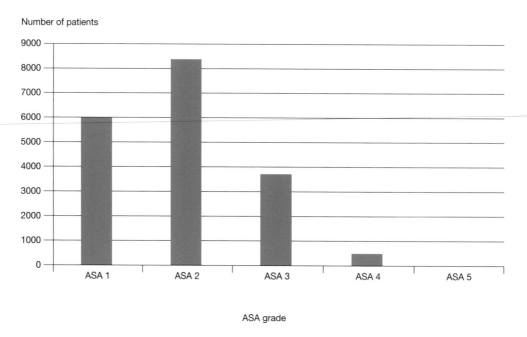

Figure 3.2 ASA Grade

Number of patients

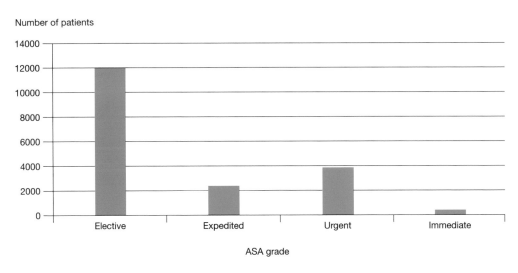

ASA grade

Figure 3.3 Urgency of surgery

Urgency of surgery was classified using the NCEPOD classification[22]. Figure 3.3 summarises this. 65% of the total population was categorised as elective, 13% as expedited, 21% as urgent and 1.5% as immediate.

Data on specific comorbidities were collected. Figure 3.4 shows this for the total population.

In total there were 10890 comorbidities documented. Many patients may have had more than one comorbidity; however, the total number of comorbidities may be a higher than expected finding given that nearly 80% of the total population was ASA 1 and 2.

Number of patients

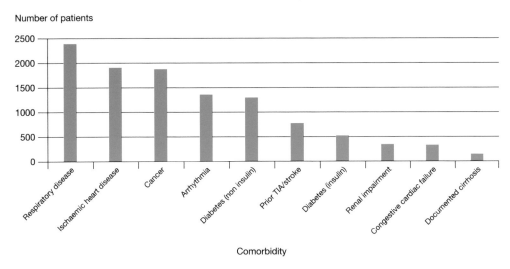

Comorbidity

Figure 3.4 Comorbidities

Postoperative location is shown in Table 3.3. Almost 7% of the total population went to a critical care unit (level 2 or 3 care) immediately after theatre or from the recovery room.

The anaesthetist returning the data was asked if the actual discharge location for the patient was ideal. Table 3.4 shows that in 353/16350 (2.1%) cases the location was thought not to be.

3.2 Outcome at 30 days post operation

In Appendix 2 there is information and discussion about 6 month outcome. For the purpose of the data in this report all outcome data refers to 30 day outcome.

The overall mortality rate at 30 days was 1.6% (displayed later in Table 3.27).

Thirty day mortality for patients was broken down by whether or not discharge location was judged to be ideal. Where there were concerns over discharge location, mortality at 30 days was 5.0% compared to 1.4% where there were no concerns over discharge location (Table 3.5).

Table 3.3 Postoperative location

Postoperative location	Number of patients	%
Recovery to ward	16128	93.3
HDU/ICU	1167	6.7
Subtotal	**17295**	
Other	79	
Not answered	1723	
Total	**19097**	

Table 3.4 Location suitable for the patient – anaesthetists' view

Discharge location ideal	Number of patients	%
Yes	16350	97.9
No	353	2.1
Subtotal	**16703**	
Not answered	2394	
Total	**19097**	

Table 3.5 Postoperative local suitable and outcome

Discharge location ideal	Alive	Deceased	% mortality	Total
Yes	11337	166	1.4	**11503**
No	248	13	5.0	**261**
Subtotal	**11585**	**179**	**1.5**	**11764**
Not answered	1714	35	2.0	**1749**
Total	**13299**	**214**	**1.6**	**13513**

Table 3.6 Outcome at 30 days by comorbidities

Comorbidities	30 day outcome			
	Alive	Deceased	% mortality	Total
Respiratory disease	1743	67	3.7	1810
Ischaemic heart disease	1402	55	3.8	1457
Cancer	1363	54	3.8	1417
Arrhythmia	970	59	5.7	1029
Diabetes (non insulin)	976	29	2.9	1005
Transient ischaemic attack (TIA)/Stroke	565	26	4.4	591
Diabetes (insulin)	370	16	4.1	386
Congestive cardiac failure	223	20	8.2	243
Documented cirrhosis	112	11	8.9	123

Patients can have multiple comorbidities and no attempt has been made to adjust for this in this analysis. However it is worth noting the association that these comorbidities have on 30 day survival status – 9% of patients with documented liver cirrhosis and 8% of patients with congestive cardiac failure died within 30 days of surgery (Table 3.6).

3.3 Risk

As stated in the introduction the high risk surgical patient group raises a number of challenges. It is known that a relatively small proportion of patients contribute to the vast majority of postoperative deaths and consume a disproportionate amount of health care resource. The identification of this group of patients can be based on patient characteristics and operative characteristics, either using clinician identification or based on scoring systems.

As stated earlier the anaesthetist caring for the patient was asked to categorise the patients as high risk or low risk at the time of anaesthesia. No guidance was given as to what classified high risk and the outcome of the patient was not know at the time of classification.

Table 3.7 Anaesthetists' views of whether the patients were high risk

High risk	Number of patients	%
Yes	3734	20.1
No	14831	79.9
Subtotal	18565	
Not answered	532	
Total	19097	

Table 3.7 shows that 20% of the patient population was considered by the anaesthetist caring for the patient to be high risk. This pragmatic approach has limitations but also advantages. The categorisation of risk was by the individual clinician and in the setting of their institution – this identification would be expected to initiate strategies to mitigate the risk, if these were available.

There was a clear difference in age between the high and low risk groups as can be seen in Figure 3.5.

Figure 3.6 shows that there was a clear increase in the perception of risk with increasing age – almost 40% of the population greater than 70 years of age was considered high risk and almost 50% of the population greater than 80 years was considered to be high risk.

Figure 3.7 shows that just over half of all comorbidities were found in the high risk group (despite the high risk group only representing 20% of the total study population).

In addition it is worth remembering the association that was shown earlier (Table 3.7 of comorbidities and outcome) and considering whether patients with certain comorbidities, that have such a high 30 day mortality, can truly be classified as low risk.

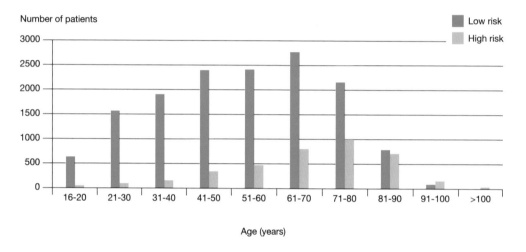

Figure 3.5 Risk group by age

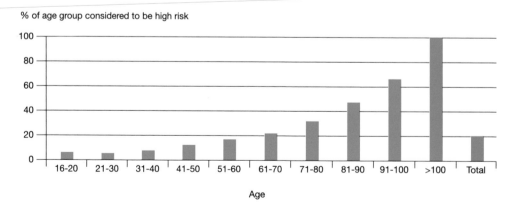

Figure 3.6 Percentage of age groups considered to be high risk

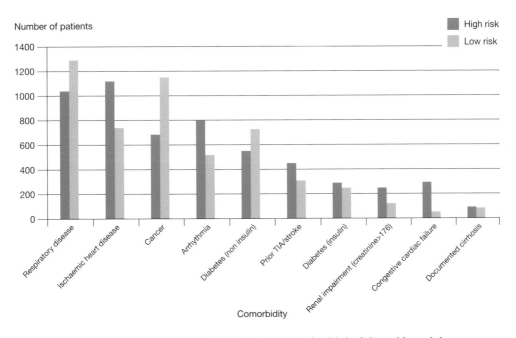

Figure 3.7 Distribution of comorbidities between the high risk and low risk groups

The urgency of surgery profile for the total population was shown earlier. This revealed that 65% of cases were elective, 12% expedited, 21% urgent and 2% immediate.

Figure 3.8 shows these data split by risk and Table 3.8 gives the absolute numbers in each group.

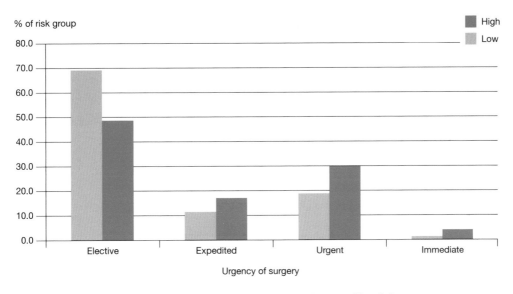

Figure 3.8 Urgency of operation displayed by risk

Table 3.8 Absolute numbers for the urgency of operation by risk

| Urgency of surgery | Risk | | | | Total |
	Low	High	Subtotal	Not answered	
Immediate	127	149	**276**	3	**279**
Urgent	2640	1096	**3736**	100	**3836**
Expedited	1681	624	**2305**	40	**2345**
Elective	10048	1774	**11822**	250	**12072**
Subtotal	**14496**	**3643**	18139	393	18532
Not answered	335	91	**426**	139	**565**
Total	**14831**	**3734**	18565	**532**	**19097**

Whilst there was a shift towards more urgent classification in the high risk group this was not as pronounced as may be thought. Of the high risk group 49% were elective, 17% expedited, 30% urgent and 4% immediate (Figure 3.8).

An alternative way to analyse urgency and risk is to look at the risk profile of each category of urgency. This is shown in Figure 3.9.

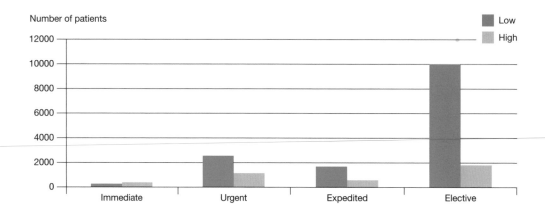

Figure 3.9 Risk profile of each category of urgency of operation

Of the 276 patients classified as immediate, 54% were thought to be high risk.
Of the 3736 patients classified as urgent, 29% were thought to be high risk.
Of the 2305 patients classified as expedited, 27% were thought to be high risk.
Of the 11822 patients classified as elective, 15% were thought to be high risk.

There are, perhaps, marked findings at both ends of the urgency spectrum – only half of the immediate patients (definition of immediate - Immediate life, limb or organ-saving intervention – resuscitation simultaneous with intervention, normally within minutes of decision to operate) were considered high risk and that as many as 15% of elective patients were thought to be high risk.

As shown previously just less than 80% of the total study population was ASA grade 1 and 2, and this figure dropped to 22% of the high risk group. As can be seen there was a relationship between ASA grade and risk, in that greater proportions of higher ASA grades were considered to be high risk (Table 3.9). However, the sensitivity of ASA grading as a risk stratification tool is not high, meaning that there were still substantial numbers of patients with a lower ASA grade who were considered to be high risk.

Table 3.10 shows the relationship between ASA grade and risk category broken down by urgency of procedure. As previously shown 1.3% of the ASA 1 patients were high risk. What is clear from Table 3.10 below is that the highest proportion of these patients was in the immediate and urgent categories. However this relationship was not seen with the ASA 3 and 4 groups where the proportion of each surgical category classed as high risk varied little.

These data allow better understanding of the complex arrangements of patient factors and operative urgency when trying to classify the degree of risk faced by a patient.

Table 3.9 ASA grade and assessment of risk

ASA Grade	High Risk				Not answered	Total
	No	Yes	Subtotal	% ASA grade high risk		
ASA 1	5800	75	5875	1.3	102	5977
ASA 2	7474	745	8219	9.1	187	8406
ASA 3	1248	2362	3610	65.4	112	3722
ASA 4	16	455	471	96.6	13	484
ASA 5	0	33	33	100.0	0	33
Subtotal	14538	3670	18208	20.2	414	18622
Not answered	293	64	357	17.9	118	475
Total	14831	3734	18565	20.1	532	19097

Table 3.10 ASA grade and risk group displayed by urgency of procedure

ASA Grade	Immediate		Urgent		Expedited		Elective		Total
	High Risk	Low Risk	High Risk	Low Risk	High Risk	Low Risk	High Risk	Low Risk	
1	15 (18.8)	65	28 (2.2)	1243	9 (1.4)	626	22 (0.6)	3745	5753
2	17 (25.0)	51	136 (11.0)	1100	96 (10.5)	817	471 (8.1)	5335	8023
3	40 (83.3)	8	681 (73.4)	247	416 (67.1)	204	1171 (60.5)	763	3530
4	52 (100)	0	216 (97.7)	5	94 (96.9)	3	83 (91.2)	8	461
5	24 (100)	0	9 (100)	0	0	0	0	0	33
Total	148 (54.4)	124	1070 (29.2)	2595	615 (27.2)	1650	1747 (15.1)	9851	17800

Table 3.11 Pre-operative assessment clinics by risk group

Pre-assessment	Low risk	%	High risk	%	Subtotal	Not answered	Total
Yes	6881	82.4	1309	78.2	8190	152	8342
No	1923	17.6	279	21.8	2202	31	2233
Subtotal	8804		1588		10392	183	10575
Not answered	700		109		809	48	857
Unknown	544		77		621	19	640
Total	10048		1774		11822	250	12072

Pre-operative assessment

One of the key components to improving outcome for high risk patients is to recognise and treat any reversible comorbidity. In addition identifying patients early allows for a discussion about treatment options and the care pathway that is required. One opportunity for this to be initiated is the pre-operative assessment clinic. Usage of these clinics will be influenced by urgency of procedure proposed. Table 3.11 shows the usage of pre-operative assessment clinics in low and high risk elective patients.

Approximately 80% of patients overall were seen in a pre-operative assessment clinic. There appears to have been a slightly greater use of pre-operative assessment clinics in the high risk group but there were still almost 18% of high risk patients not assessed in a clinic before admission.

3.4 The surgery undertaken

Table 3.12 Summary of the type of surgery undertaken

Type of surgery	Number of patients	%
Intra abdominal	2963	21.9
Intra thoracic	157	1.2
Both	28	0.2
Neither	10365	76.7
Total	13513	

Of the patients included in the study 22% had intra abdominal surgery whilst 1% had intra thoracic surgery (Table 3.12).

Table 3.13 shows the breakdown of surgical category by risk group.

Table 3.13 Type of surgery by risk group

Type of surgery	Risk				Not answered	Total
	Low	High	% of group high risk	Subtotal		
Intra abdominal	2212	682	23.6	2894	69	2963
Intra thoracic	88	63	41.7	151	6	157
Both	13	15	53.6	28	0	28
Neither	8198	1908	18.9	10106	259	10365
Total	10511	2668	20.2	13179	334	13513

The number of patients undergoing intra thoracic surgery was low, but just under a half of this group was considered high risk. Patients undergoing intra abdominal surgery were thought to be high risk in almost a quarter of cases. The remaining surgery (i.e. not including body cavities) made up the bulk of surgical activity and was considered high risk in almost a fifth of cases. It is often perceived that intra abdominal surgery makes up a significant proportion of high risk cases but within this study that effect did not seem especially pronounced.

Different surgical procedures are associated with different clinical outcomes.

Table 3.14 shows this relationship for all patients within the study period.

There was a small increase in 30 day mortality for the patients undergoing intra abdominal or intra thoracic surgery compared with surgery not including body cavities. There was a small group of patients who had surgical procedures in both the abdominal and thoracic cavities. Whilst the numbers are small it is intuitive that such major surgery may be associated with a high mortality rate and these data support this.

Urgency of operation is also an important variable in outcome following surgery. The following Tables show outcome data for surgical category for both elective and non-elective (immediate, urgent and expedited) patients.

Table 3.14 Type of surgery by outcome

Type of surgery	Outcome		% mortality	Total
	Alive	Deceased		
Intra abdominal	2892	71	2.4	2963
Intra thoracic	153	4	2.5	157
Both	23	5	17.9	28
Neither	10231	134	1.3	10365
Total	**13299**	**214**	**1.6**	**13513**

Table 3.15 Outcome of elective surgery

Type of surgery	Outcome		% mortality	Total
	Alive	Deceased		
Intra abdominal	1713	15	0.9	1728
Intra thoracic	87	1	1.1	88
Both	13	3	18.8	16
Neither	6784	12	0.2	6796
Total	**8597**	**31**	**0.4**	**8628**

Table 3.16 Outcome of non-elective surgery

Type of surgery	Outcome		% mortality	Total
	Alive	Deceased		
Intra abdominal	1118	55	4.7	1173
Intra thoracic	64	3	4.5	67
Both	10	2	16.7	12
Neither	3154	118	3.6	3272
Total	**4346**	**178**	**3.9**	**4524**

Table 3.17 Outcome of non-elective intra abdominal surgery by urgency

Urgency of surgery	Outcome		% mortality	Total
	Alive	Deceased		
Immediate	76	12	13.6	88
Urgent	687	37	5.1	724
Expedited	355	6	1.7	361
Total	**1118**	**55**	**4.7**	**1173**

Table 3.18 Outcome for high risk elective surgery by type of surgery

Type of surgery	Outcome		% mortality	Total
	Alive	Deceased		
Intra abdominal	310	9	2.8	319
Intra thoracic	30	1	3.2	31
Both	6	1	14.3	7
Neither	956	7	0.7	963
Total	**1302**	**18**	**1.4**	**1320**

Table 3.19 Outcome for high risk non-elective surgery by type of surgery

Type of surgery	Outcome		% mortality	Total
	Alive	Deceased		
Intra abdominal	303	46	13.2	349
Intra thoracic	29	2	6.5	31
Both	6	2	25.0	8
Neither	800	94	10.5	894
Total	**1138**	**144**	**11.2**	**1282**

As can be seen, non-elective patients had a higher mortality rate than elective patients. In patients undergoing intra abdominal surgery there was a fivefold increase in mortality for non elective cases.

The non-elective, intra abdominal cases are further broken down in Table 3.17.

This illustrates that urgency is strongly linked with outcome for this group with both urgent and immediate categories having substantial increases in mortality compared with expedited or elective patients.

Tables 3.18 and 3.19 show data for surgical category for both elective and non-elective (immediate, urgent and expedited) for patients assessed by clinicians as high risk.

Whilst the literature tells us that the high risk surgical population has an overall mortality rate of approximately 10% it is intuitive that there will be some groups of patients with much poorer outcomes. The data in Tables 3.18 & 3.19 suggests that high risk, non-elective patients have a worse outcome and within that group intra abdominal surgery appears to be a particular issue.

Table 3.20 presents that data for all intra abdominal operations and emphasises that the high risk group who have intra abdominal procedures have a greater mortality rate (3% absolute increase over non intra abdominal procedures).

Table 3.21 presents a further analysis of the 2922 patients who had intra abdominal surgery and splits them by whether gut resection was part of the surgical procedure. These data are for all patients (both elective and non-elective). This data show that those patients who had a gut resection had a greater mortality than those who did not have a gut resection (gut resection 32/588 (5%) v no gut resection 36/2151 (1.7%). In addition patients identified as high risk, who underwent a gut resection, had a 1 in 10 chance of dying within 30 days of operation.

Table 3.20 Outcome of intra abdominal surgery by risk group

	Risk						
	Low			High			
Intra abdominal surgery	Alive	Deceased	% mortality	Alive	Deceased	% mortality	Total
Yes	2209	16	0.7	638	59	8.5	2922
No	8259	27	0.3	1865	106	5.4	10257
Total	10468	43	0.4	2503	165	6.2	13179

Table 3.21 Outcome of gut resection surgery by risk group

	Risk						
	Low			High			
Gut resection	Alive	Deceased	% mortality	Alive	Deceased	% mortality	Total
Yes	355	7	1.9	201	25	11.1	588
No	1729	9	0.5	386	27	6.5	2151
Not answered	125	0	0.0	51	7	12.1	183
Total	2209	16	0.7	638	59	8.5	2922

Table 3.22 Outcome of gut resection surgery and a primary anastomosis by risk group

| Primary anastomosis | Risk | | | | | | | Total |
| | Low | | | High | | | | |
	Alive	Deceased	% mortality	Alive	Deceased	% mortality		
Yes	229	5	2.1	126	10	7.4		370
No	56	2	3.4	39	10	20.4		107
Not answered	70	0	0.0	36	5	12.2		111
Total	**355**	**7**	**1.9**	**201**	**25**	**11.1**		**588**

Table 3.22 shows a further analysis of the 588 patients who had a gut resection, and looks at whether a primary anastomosis was performed as part of the procedure.

Both low and high risk patients had poorer outcomes if a primary anastomosis was not part of the surgical procedure. This is probably a reflection of physiology and surgical findings as the group having non-anastomosing surgery are likely to be sicker with different surgical pathology.

Monitoring

In addition to minimal monitoring standards that exist [23] it is likely that some patients may benefit from additional information that can be gained from more advanced haemodynamic monitoring. Table 3.23 shows the usage of arterial lines, central lines and cardiac output monitoring in the study population.

Table 3.23 Percentage of each group with monitoring modality

Monitoring	All cases	High Risk	Low Risk
Arterial catheter	8.9	26.6	4.3
Central venous catheter	4.3	14.2	1.9
Cardiac output monitoring	2.2	4.7	1.6

It can be seen in Table 3.23 that there was a greater usage of arterial lines and central venous lines in the high risk group; although the usage was still only 1 in 4 for arterial lines in high risk patients and 1 in 7 for central venous lines in high risk patients. The use of cardiac output monitoring was very low in the study with a slight increase in the high risk group despite evidence for use of cardiac output monitoring. In addition there has been recent NICE guidance to support the use of cardiac output monitoring[13] but this practice had not become widely adopted by the time of this study.

Postoperative location

It was shown earlier that 6.7% (1167/17295) of the total study population went to a critical care unit immediately after theatre or recovery room. Table 3.24 shows these data for the high risk population.

Table 3.24 Postoperative location for high risk patients

Postoperative location	Number of patients	%
Recovery to ward	2587	77.9
HDU/ICU	736	22.1
Subtotal	**3323**	
Other	26	
Not answered	385	
Total	**3734**	

In addition 403/13596 (2.9%) low risk patients went to a critical care unit immediately after theatre or recovery room. It appears that there was some streaming of the high risk patients towards a critical care pathway. However, for the majority of high risk patients (almost 4 out of 5) the pathway was to return to a level 1 ward immediately after theatre or recovery room. This low percentage of patients accessing a critical care unit may have many reasons: lack of awareness of the degree of risk, lack of belief that a critical care pathway will improve outcome, acceptance of current pathways and limitations of current availability of critical care beds, to name a few. In the context of availability of critical care beds the 403 low risk patients who utilised this facility should be considered. Would these resources have been better used for the high risk group and would outcomes be improved if we used our resources more effectively by admitting only the higher risk patients?

Whether the patient is admitted to a critical care unit or a ward immediately after theatre or recovery room appeared to be influenced by urgency of surgery (Table 3.25).

As previously shown 22% of all high risk patients had an immediate pathway through a critical care unit. The figure is slightly lower for elective high risk patients and slightly higher for urgent and expedited high risk patients. However, the immediate high risk patients had a three fold greater usage of critical care facilities in the immediate postoperative phase.

At the time of discharge from theatre, the anaesthetist was asked if they were content with the discharge location. As shown earlier in 353 cases (2%) there were concerns about discharge location. Table 3.26 shows the data for these patients analysed by risk.

Table 3.25 Type of ward by urgency of surgery - high risk patients

| Urgency of surgery | Type of ward | | | | | | | |
	Recovery to ward	%	Critical care	%	Subtotal	Other	Not answered	Total
Immediate	48	35.8	86	64.2	134	6	9	149
Urgent	759	77.3	223	22.7	982	11	103	1100
Expedited	416	76.1	131	23.9	547	3	74	626
Elective	1299	82.2	281	17.8	1580	6	188	1777
Subtotal	2522	77.8	721	22.2	3243	26	374	3643
Not answered	65	81.3	15	18.8	80	0	11	91
Total	2587	77.9	736	22.1	3323	26	385	3734

Table 3.26 Postoperative location suitable in the anaesthetists' opinion by risk group

| Discharge location ideal | High risk | | Low risk | |
	Number of patients	%	Number of patients	%
Yes	3000	93.9	13012	98.9
No	195	6.1	150	1.1
Subtotal	3195		13162	
Not answered	539		1669	
Total	3734		14831	

Most of the concerns about discharge location were in the high risk group and the clinicians felt that they should mostly have gone to a higher level of care.

Outcome data by risk categorisation

Mortality at 30 days in the whole study population was 1.6% (214/13513). Table 3.27 shows 30 day outcome detailed by risk category.

The clinician's prospective classification of risk appears to have described two groups of patients with quite different outcomes. The mortality in the high risk group was 6.2%. This is slightly lower than the estimates in the literature (where mortality rates of 10-12% are quoted). It may be that the groups are different and that the clinicians included some lower risk patients in the high risk group. Given that 20% of patients were classified as high risk this may be the case. Further data on peer review of high risk cases and alternative ways of presenting risk is shown in Chapters 1 and 4.

Of the 214 deaths at 30 days, 166 (77%) were in the high risk group. The fact that most of the deaths are within the high risk group is in keeping with the published literature. These data emphasise that it was possible to identify a group of patients with poor outcomes and also that the vast majority of postoperative deaths were in this group. There was no attempt to collect morbidity data but the literature suggests that this group also have the burden of significant morbidity and consume disproportionate resources.

There was a relationship between urgency and outcome. Table 3.28 shows the urgency group alive and deceased at 30 days.

Table 3.28 Urgency of procedure by outcome at 30 days post operation

Urgency of surgery	30 day outcome		
	Alive	Deceased	%
Immediate	164	24	12.8
Urgent	2566	117	4.4
Expedited	1616	37	2.2
Elective	8597	31	<1
Subtotal	**12943**	**209**	
Not answered	356	5	
Total	**13299**	**214**	

Thirty day mortality was 13% for immediate, 4% for urgent, 2% for expedited and 0.4% for elective operations.

This relationship between urgency and mortality is shown in Table 3.29, and is also presented for the high and low risk groups. The figures are percentages of each group who had died at 30 days.

Table 3.27 Outcome at 30 days post operation by risk

30 day outcome	Risk				All (%)
	Low (%)	High (%)	Subtotal	Not answered	
Alive	10468	2503	**12971**	328	13299
Deceased	43 (0.4)	165 (6.2)	**208**	6	214 (1.6)
Total	**10511**	**2668**	**13179**	**334**	**13513**

Table 3.29 Mortality by risk group and urgency of surgery

Urgency of surgery	Risk		
	Low	High	All
Immediate	1.1	24.2	12.8
Urgent	1.1	12.6	4.3
Expedited	0.7	6.2	2.2
Elective	0.2	1.4	0.4

As can be seen urgency in high risk patients is closely linked to mortality. One quarter of high risk, immediate patients had died at 30 days. The figure for urgent and expedited high risk patients was 1 in 8 and 1 in 16 respectively.

As shown previously only 80% of elective patients were seen in a pre-admission assessment clinic prior to their operation and this was not different for the high and low risk groups.

4.8% for those seen and not seen in a pre-admission clinic (Table 3.30). The corresponding outcome data for expedited patients is 2.4% v 9.4%. It appears that 30 day mortality is substantially lower in high risk patients who are seen in a pre-operative assessment clinic.

It may be that many factors explain this apparent large effect of pre-admission clinics and outcome. Modification of comorbidities may improve outcome for patients who subsequently undergo an operation. Alternatively the very high risk patients seen in pre-assessment clinics may be declined an operation – thus lowering the mortality in the group that do subsequently undergo an operation.

Table 3.30 Use of pre-admission assessment clinics in high risk patients.

Urgency of surgery	Seen in a pre-assessment clinic						
	Yes			No			
	Alive	Deceased	% mortality	Alive	Deceased	% mortality	Total
Immediate	1	0	0.0	61	20	24.7	82
Urgent	52	2	3.7	518	81	13.5	653
Expedited	166	4	2.4	212	22	9.4	404
Elective	991	7	0.7	178	9	4.8	1185
Total	**1210**	**13**	**1.1**	**969**	**132**	**12.0**	**2324**

It is difficult to interpret these data for immediate and urgent patients. However, for the elective and expedited group there should have been an opportunity to stream patients through an appropriate pre-admission assessment clinic. In these latter two categories it can be seen that the patients who were not seen in a pre-assessment clinic had a poorer survival at 30 days. Mortality at 30 days for elective patients was 0.7% v

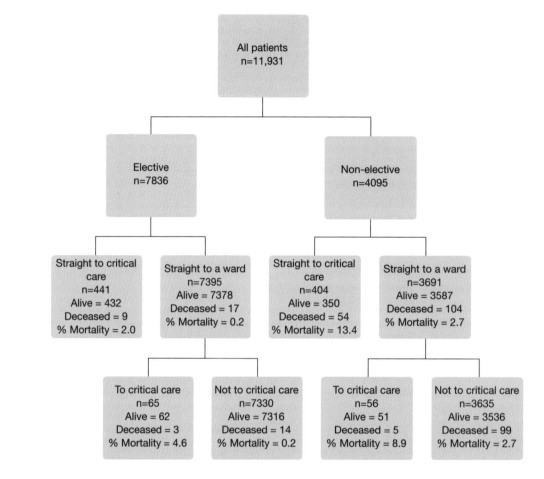

Figure 3.10 shows the critical care usage for all patients

Critical care utilisation

From Figure 3.10 it can be seen that only 966/11931 (8.1%) patients had a pathway that included admission to a critical care unit. 845/11931 (7.1%) were admitted to a critical care unit directly from theatre/recovery whilst 127/11801 (1.0%) had an admission to critical care after a period of ward stay.

These data reveal some interesting findings.

1. Patients who were not initially admitted to critical care but had a subsequent admission after a period of ward stay had poor outcome. For elective patients in the whole population the 30 day mortality was 4.6% v 0.2% (later admission v no admission). For non-elective patients the corresponding outcome data was 8.9% v 2.7%.

2. 74 high risk non-elective patients were returned to ward care after surgery and died without escalation to a higher level of care. The 30 day mortality rate of this group (i.e. high risk, non-elective, ward care only) was 9.1%.

3. 31 low risk patients were returned to ward care after surgery and died without escalation to a higher level of care.

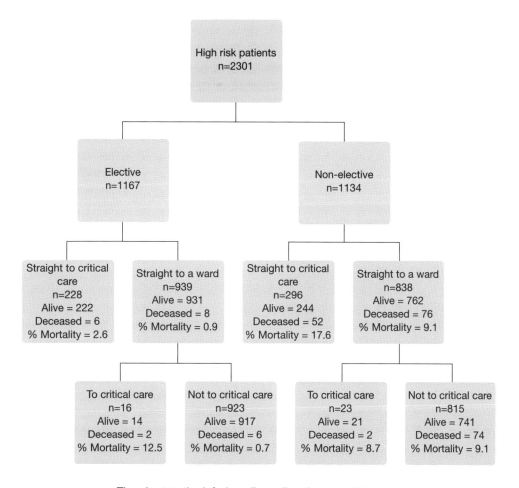

The chart to the left describes all patients and the chart above describes high risk patients

These data support the argument that there are a number of patients who can be identified as being at high risk for poor outcomes, but that their postoperative needs are not well met. Furthermore if the postoperative critical care is delivered later on in the postoperative period, presumably after deterioration, the outcome for these patients is much worse.

Table 3.31 gives data on all patients who died (high and low risk) who did not have a critical care period. Of the 214 deaths within 30 days of surgery, 114 did not have a critical care period (53%).

Table 3.31 All patients who died who did not have a critical care episode

Urgency of surgery	Number of patients
Immediate	3
Urgent	70
Expedited	25
Elective	14
Not answered	2
Total	**114**

As stated before 79% of postoperative deaths were in the high risk group (165/208).

Of these 165 patients, 80 died without ever being admitted to a critical care unit. Of these 80 patients the breakdown by urgency of operation is shown in Table 3.32.

Table 3.32 High risk patients who died who did not have a critical care episode

Urgency of surgery	Number of patients
Elective	6
Expedited	18
Urgent	53
Immediate	2
Subtotal	**79**
Not answered	1
Total	**80**

Data were not collected to explore the reasons for the lack of critical care admission to support an operative package of care. There may well have been intra-operative findings that dictated survival was not possible and a palliative pathway was put in place. It is unlikely that this would account for all the patients above, particularly the elective and expedited categories, but we did not collect data to determine this aspect of management.

This raises the question about appropriate case planning and ensuring that all required elements are available and utilised, to ensure best outcomes. There is a perception that in some cases an operation is undertaken but a decision has been made that it would not be reasonable to include critical care support in that case. This does not seem sensible as a simple level 2 critical care stay may well improve outcome, both morbidity and mortality. Is this an example of clinicians perpetuating a self fulfilling prophecy? Is practice dictated by the limited availability of critical care beds and have clinicians become accepting of this situation?

Key Findings - Prospective data

Anaesthetists involved in the surgery identified 3734/18565 patients as high risk (20%).

79% of the deaths were in the high risk group (165/208).

Urgency of surgery did not correlate well with risk category – half of the high risk patients were elective procedures.

Higher ASA grades had a higher proportion of high risk patients – however there were still substantial numbers of high risk patients in ASA grades 1-2.

Almost 1 in 5 elective high risk patients were not seen in a pre-assessment clinic. Within this study, elective patients not seen in a pre-admission assessment clinic had a higher 30 day mortality than those who were seen (4.8% v 0.7%).

Arterial lines, central lines and cardiac output monitoring were only used in 27%, 14% and 5% of the high risk group. This is despite the considerable evidence that peri-operative haemodynamic monitoring can improve patient outcomes.

Overall mortality at 30 days was 1.6%. The mortality in the high risk group was 6.2% and in the low risk group was 0.4%.

Degree of surgical urgency in high risk patients was closely linked to mortality. 1 in 4 high risk, immediate patients were deceased at 30 days. The figure for urgent and expedited high risk patients was 1 in 8 and 1 in 16 respectively.

1167/17295 (6.7%) of patients were cared for in a critical care unit immediately after theatre/recovery. In the high risk group this figure was 736/3323 (22.1%), returning almost 4 out of 5 of the high risk population to ward level care.

There were concerns over postoperative location (from theatre/recovery) in 353 cases. These cases had a 30 day mortality rate of 5.0 % compared to 1.4% where there were no concerns.

48% of high risk patients who died never went to a critical care facility (80/165).

14/26 elective and 99/158 non-elective patients who died never accessed critical care facilities.

Recommendations

There is a need to introduce a UK wide system that allows rapid and easy identification of patients who are at high risk of postoperative mortality and morbidity. (Departments of Health in England, Wales & Northern Ireland)

The decision to operate on high risk patients (particularly non-elective) should be made at consultant level, involving surgeons and those who will provide intra and postoperative care. (Clinical Directors and Consultants)

An assessment of mortality risk should be made explicit to the patient and recorded clearly on the consent form and in the medical record. (Consultants)

Once a decision to operate has been made there is a need to provide a package of full supportive care. This may include critical care admission or support, for the higher risk patients. If critical care admission is not possible then the decision to operate is being made without provision of an appropriate package of care: this should be communicated to the patient as part of the consent procedure. (Clinical Directors and Consultants)

Better intra-operative monitoring for high risk patients is required. The evidence base supports the use of peri-operative optimisation and this relies on extended haemodynamic monitoring. NICE Medical Technology Guidance 3 relating to cardiac output monitoring should be applied. (Clinical Directors)

The postoperative care of the high risk surgical patient needs to be improved. Each Trust must make provision for sufficient critical care beds or pathways of care to provide appropriate support in the postoperative period. (Medical Directors)

To aid planning for provision of facilities for high risk patients, each Trust should analyse the volume of work considered to be high risk and quantify the critical care requirements of this cohort. This assessment and plan should be reported to the Trust Board on an annual basis. (Medical Directors)

This peer review section focuses on a sample of cases taken from the original prospective dataset of 19097 cases. The cases were sampled from the population in the prospective data set who were designated as high risk (3734 cases) by the attending anaesthetists. Peer review of these patients provided a qualitative review of their care and complements the quantitative data already produced. This is in line with established NCEPOD methodology looking for areas of patient care that might be improved.

As stated earlier the stratification of risk could have been based on patient comorbidities, age, urgency of surgery and procedure performed. However, for the purpose of this study the anaesthetists, who filled out the prospective data collection form, were asked whether they considered the patient to be high risk. No definition of what constituted a high risk patient was

provided and this classification was therefore shaped by the anaesthetists' knowledge of the high risk surgical literature and their own perception of risk in the context of their own institutions. The reasons for this pragmatic definition were discussed earlier. Subsequently, 829 high risk cases were peer reviewed by the Advisors.

4.1 Descriptive data

The age range of the peer reviewed group was 16-101 years (mean of 68 years, standard deviation of 16). Figure 4.1 displays the percentage of age ranges on the peer review group against the prospective data. 409/829 patients (49%) were female. The peer reviewed group of high risk patients trended towards the higher age groups.

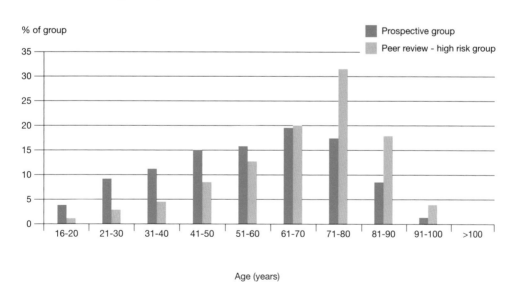

Figure 4.1 Age range of the peer review group compared to the prospective group

47

Height and weight was used to calculate body mass index (BMI). These data are given below in Table 4.1 for the peer reviewed data set.

These BMI data are similar for the prospective set of patients. It is a sign of society as a whole that 66% of patients operated on in a single week were considered to be overweight.

As can be seen only 214/739 (29%) patients were in the BMI range 18-25, which is considered to be the normal range. 30 patients were underweight and the majority, 495/739 (67%) patients were overweight. The proportion of patients with a BMI of over 25 was similar in the prospective data set where 66.2% of patients were overweight. These figures are in line with national

data from 2008 which showed 66% of men and 57% of women were classified as overweight[24].

The ASA grade of the sample is shown in Table 4.2. 24% of the sample was considered to be ASA 1 or 2. The peer reviewed group also had a greater proportion of patients in ASA groups 3, 4 and 5 and far lower proportions of patients in ASA 1 and 2.

Comorbidities are shown in Table 4.3. Comorbidities were frequent in the whole prospective data set but the incidence was much higher in the peer reviewed group (1203 comorbidities in 829 peer reviewed patients [1.5 comorbidities per patient] compared with 10890 comorbidities in 19097 patients [0.6 comorbidities per patient]). The three commonest comorbidities were ischaemic heart disease, respiratory disease and arrhythmias.

Table 4.1 BMI of the peer reviewed data set

BMI	Prospective		Peer review	
	Number of patients	%	Number of patients	%
<16.5	71	0.4	10	1.4
16.5 – 18.49	238	1.4	20	2.7
18.5 – 24.99	5313	32.0	214	29.0
25 – 29.99	6013	36.2	219	29.6
30 – 34.99	2977	17.9	120	16.2
35 – 39.99	1195	7.2	68	9.2
≥ 40	807	4.9	88	11.9
Subtotal	16614		739	
Weight or height not provided	2483		90	
Total	19097		829	

Urgency of surgery was classified using the NCEPOD classification. Table 4.4 shows the breakdown: 55% of the peer reviewed population was categorised as elective, 16% as expedited, 26% as urgent and 4% as immediate. The urgency profile for the peer review group had a lower proportion of elective patients and a higher proportion of urgent patients than the total population.

Table 4.2 ASA grade in the peer review dataset against the prospective group

ASA Grade	Prospective		Peer reviewed	
	Number of patients	%	Number of patients	%
ASA 1	5977	32.1	21	2.6
ASA 2	8406	45.1	171	20.9
ASA 3	3722	20.0	537	65.6
ASA 4	484	2.6	83	10.1
ASA 5	33	<1	7	<1
Subtotal	18622		819	
Not answered	475		10	
Total	19097		829	

Table 4.3 Comorbidities in the peer review dataset against the prospective group

Comorbidities	Prospective		Peer reviewed	
	Number of patients	%	Number of patients	%
Respiratory disease	2371	12.4	230	27.7
Ischaemic heart disease	1894	9.9	254	30.6
Cancer	1862	9.8	138	16.6
Arrhythmia	1342	7.0	169	20.4
Diabetes (non insulin)	1286	6.7	129	15.6
Prior TIA/stroke	762	4.0	101	12.2
Diabetes (insulin)	530	2.8	53	6.4
Renal impairment (creatinine >176mmol/L)	348	1.8	42	5.1
Congestive cardiac failure	333	1.7	67	8.1
Documented cirrhosis	162	<1	20	2.4

Table 4.4 Urgency of surgery in the peer review dataset against the prospective group

Urgency of surgery	Prospective		Peer reviewed	
	Number of patients	%	Number of patients	%
Immediate	279	1.5	29	3.6
Urgent	3836	20.7	211	26.2
Expedited	2345	12.7	127	15.8
Elective	12072	65.1	439	54.5
Subtotal	18532		806	
Not answered	565		23	
Total	19097		829	

Table 4.5 Mortality for elective and non-elective patients

Urgency of surgery	30 day outcome			
	Alive	Deceased	% mortality	Total
Elective	542	8	1.5	550
Non-elective	217	48	18.1	265
Subtotal	759	56	6.9	815
Not answered	13	1	7.1	14
Total	772	57	6.9	829

These findings of older age groupings, higher ASA grades, higher rates of comorbidities and more urgent surgery are to be expected in the peer reviewed group as age, ASA, comorbidity and urgency of surgery are all associated with risk. However, it is reassuring to note the presence of these factors and this gives confidence that the group of patients who were selected for peer review do represent a higher risk group compared to the total population.

4.2 Outcome data of the peer review group

The mortality rate at 30 days postoperatively was 6.9% (57/829 patients). This is in line with the mortality rate for all the high risk cases within the prospective data set (166/2684 – 6.2%). It is however lower than the literature estimates for 30 day mortality rates in the high risk population and the possible reasons for this difference have been discussed earlier.

It is no surprise that mortality is higher in non-elective patients but it is a stark fact that almost 1 in 5 non-elective patients who were prospectively identified as high risk died within 30 days of surgery (Table 4.5).

4.3 Overall assessment of care

The Advisors considered the overall care of patients and graded it as follows (Figure 4.2):

Overall the care of patients was good in only 48% (390) of high risk patients. There was room for improvement in the clinical care of 182 (20%) of patients, room for improvement in the organisational care of 91 patients and room for improvement in both in 64 patients. Overall the Advisor's believed that care was less than satisfactory in 12 patients.

Table 4.6 demonstrates the overall quality of care when the patient group was divided into elective and non-elective patients.

The standard of care delivered to elective patients was good in 58.5% of high risk patients and good in 40.3% of non-elective high risk patients. The NHS has focused on elective care in recent years and it appears that there is a need to improve the care of patients undergoing non-elective surgery.

Percentage

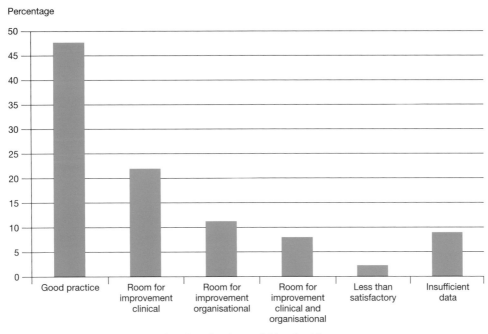

Overall quality of care - Advisors' opinion

Figure 4.2 Advisors' overall assessment of the standard of care received

Table 4.6 Overall quality of care by admission category

Overall quality of care	Elective		Non-elective	
	Number of patients	%	Number of patients	%
Good practice	296	58.5	94	40.3
Room for improvement – Clinical	114	22.5	68	29.2
Room for improvement – Organisational	59	11.7	32	13.7
Room for improvement – Clinical and Organisational	32	6.3	32	13.7
Less than satisfactory	5	1.0	7	3.0
Subtotal	**506**		**233**	
Insufficient data	44		32	
Total	**550**		**265**	

51

4.4 Risk assessment

As previously shown the anaesthetists completing the prospective data form assessed almost 20% of the study population as high risk. No guidance was issued to the clinicians returning the data. This is higher than the literature would suggest – previous research has indicated that approximately 12% of the operative population should be considered high risk. In this peer review dataset the Advisor group had the opportunity to consider the classification of risk.

The review of the high risk cases by the NCEPOD Advisors uncovered a lack of agreement between the Advisors and assessment by the supervising anaesthetists as to what constituted a high risk patient. The Advisors considered that 22.5% of elective and 14.6% of non-elective patients should not have been classified as high risk by the supervising anaesthetist at the time of operation (Tables 4.7 and 4.8). Overall, 160/802 (20%) patients were considered not to be high risk by Advisors.

An alternative and less subjective method of assessing risk is to use an established scoring system. The Lee risk index has been described earlier in Chapter 1. Table 4.9 shows Lee class for the whole peer reviewed sample and for the patients considered by the Advisors to be low risk. The percentage of high risk patients in Lee class I and II was almost 80%. However, in the group where the Advisors disagreed with the classification of high risk almost 90% were in Lee class I and II. These objective data appear to support the Advisors opinion that classification of risk was not always correct.

If this is compared back to the prospective dataset Table 4.10 shows the total number of patients in the prospective dataset for each Lee class, presented by whether or not they were identified as high risk by the anaesthetists completing the form.

Complete data were available to allow this to be calculated in 18829 patients. 3745/18829 were identified as high risk by the anaesthetist (19.9%). Using a Lee class of III or

Table 4.7 Advisors' opinion on whether the 'high risk' case was high risk in elective cases

High risk elective – Advisors' opinion	Number of patients	%
Yes	420	77.5
No	122	22.5
Subtotal	542	
Insufficient data	8	
Total	550	

Table 4.8 Advisors' opinion on whether the 'high risk' case was high risk in non-elective cases

High risk non-elective – Advisors' opinion	Number of patients	%
Yes	222	85.4
No	38	14.6
Subtotal	260	
Insufficient data	5	
Total	265	

Table 4.9 Lee class for the peer review dataset against those cases that the Advisors thought were low risk

Lee class	High risk patients Number of patients	%	Considered low risk (Advisors) Number of patients	%
I	301	36.3	80	48.8
II	360	43.4	68	41.5
III	132	15.9	13	7.9
IV	36	4.3	3	1.8
Total	**829**		**164**	

Table 4.10 Lee class for the prospective dataset against those cases that the anaesthetists thought were high risk

Lee class	High risk (anaesthetists' assessment) Yes	No	Total
I	1356	10933	**12289**
II	1600	2188	**3788**
III	615	1833	**2448**
IV	174	130	**304**
Total	**3745**	**15084**	**18829**

greater identified 2752/18829 as high risk (14.6%), a figure that is more in keeping with the available literature. Of interest is the discrepancy between clinician's assessment and Lee class (Figure 4.3).

Figure 4.3 above shows that in the group who scored Lee class I, the anaesthetists prospectively labeled 11% as high risk. With increasing Lee class there were higher proportions of patients labeled as high risk, but even in Lee class IV only 57% were classified as high risk. These data emphasise that identification of high risk patients is complex and that possibly no single method covers all possibilities.

Until a reliable method of identifying high risk patients is developed, each hospital should work towards identifying patients at risk of adverse outcomes and put in place a system to try and reduce their morbidity and mortality.

Recognising the limitations in predicting outcome it is important to be aware that a proportion of patients who have not been identified as high risk before surgery will go on to develop complications. Each hospital should ensure that there is a system to rapidly recognise and deal appropriately with postoperative deterioration.

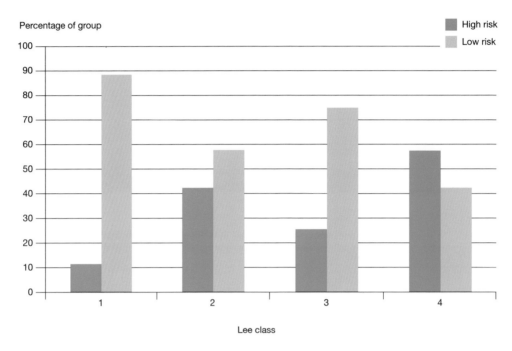

Figure 4.3 Anaesthetists view of risk against Lee class

Outcome of the peer review group by risk stratification

Shown earlier was the 30 day outcome for all patients prospectively identified as high risk by the supervising anaesthetist (Table 4.5). Further analyses of outcome for elective and non-elective patients by Advisor agreement of risk stratification are shown in Tables 4.11 & 4.12.

In the elective group there were eight cases of death (1.5%) within 30 days of surgery. In the group whom the Advisors did not agree with the classification of high risk there were no deaths and in the group where there was agreement there were eight deaths (1.9%).

Table 4.11 Outcome at 30 days for high risk elective patients

Elective patients	30 day outcome			
High risk - Advisors' opinion	Alive	Deceased	% mortality	Total
Yes	412	8	1.9	420
No	122	0	0.0	122
Subtotal	534	8	1.5	542
Not answered	8	0	0.0	8
Total	542	8	1.5	550

Table 4.12 Outcome at 30 days for high risk non-elective patients

Non-elective patients	30 day outcome			
High risk - Advisors' opinion	Alive	Deceased	% mortality	Total
Yes	178	44	19.8	222
No	35	3	7.9	38
Subtotal	213	47	18.1	260
Not answered	4	1	20.0	5
Total	217	48	18.1	265

In the non-elective group there were 48 cases of death (18.1%) within 30 days of surgery (Table 4.12). In the group whom the Advisors did not agree with the classification of high risk there were only three deaths (7.9%) and in the group where there was agreement there were 44 deaths (19.8%).

In the prospective data section we have shown that 3745/18829 patients were classified as high risk (20% of cases). This is a higher figure than the literature estimates of 10-15% of the surgical population who are considered high risk. However, if the Advisor assessment that 20% of the high risk cases that were peer reviewed were not correctly classified is applied to the total population the high risk figure would be 2996 patients (16% of cases). It is clear that risk is related to patient factors (e.g. age, comorbidities) operative factors (proposed surgical procedure) and can be a combination of both. In addition, urgency of surgery is also a contributing factor (either due to the degree of physiological insult associated with the need for urgent surgery or the lack of time to prepare the patient). Advisors were asked to apportion risk in each reviewed case to patient factors and/or the surgical procedure itself. These data are shown in Table 4.13. Overall it was felt that risk was associated with operative factors alone in 3% of cases, patient factors alone in 62% of cases and a combination of both in 35% of cases. It appears that the Advisors considered patient factors to be the most frequent reason for determination of high risk and as was shown earlier, the high risk group were older, had higher ASA grades and more comorbidities than the prospective data group.

Table 4.13 Risk attributed to patient and/or operation by the anaesthetist

Risk factors	Elective	Non-elective	Total
Patient and Operation	134	86	220
Patient	268	128	396
Operation	16	6	22
Not specified	2	2	4
Total	420	222	642

When urgency of operation was considered there were some differences. In elective patients it was felt that risk was due to patient factors in 64% of cases but in non-elective cases the corresponding figure was 58%. It was believed that a combination of patient and operative factors was the reason for classification as high risk in 32% of elective patients and 39% of non-elective patients.

What is clear from these data and the corresponding prospective data is that there was no consistency in the decision to label patients as high risk. One of the key outputs of this work must be to stimulate development of a robust, easily implemented and consistent framework to allow early identification of patients at greatest risk of peri-operative death and morbidity.

4.5 Pre-operative assessment

For the purpose of examining pre-operative assessment, patients were divided into elective and non-elective, as clearly the urgency of surgery and time prior to surgical intervention will have an effect on the process of pre-operative assessment.

In this sample 550 patients were considered to be elective admissions and 265 considered non-elective (Table 4.14).

Table 4.14 Planned admissions

Elective admission	Number of patients	%
Yes	550	67.5
No	265	32.5
Subtotal	815	
Not answered	14	
Total	829	

Preparing a patient for surgery requires an understanding of the patient's pre-operative condition, the surgery and anaesthetic techniques involved and overall risk challenging the patient. Comorbidities require careful assessment and preparation. Pre-assessment decreases cancellation on the day of surgery, improves patient's experience of surgery and may reduce complication rates and mortality[25].

Pre-operative assessment for elective admissions

Of the elective admissions only 402/515 (78%) were seen in a pre-assessment clinic (Table 4.15). Unfortunately, 113 (22%) high-risk elective patients were not seen. It is well recognised that patients benefit from pre-assessment and pre-operative planning of their hospital episode. Those who are considered to be high risk should all attend pre-assessment clinics. This level of utilisation of pre-assessment clinics was shown in the whole data set, and it is worth referring back to the prospective data (page 34) to show that there was an association with use of pre-assessment clinics and 30 day outcome. An example of such a case is shown in case study 1.

Table 4.15 Planned admissions seen in a pre-admission assessment clinic

Pre-admission assessment clinic	Number of patients	%
Yes	402	78.1
No	113	21.9
Subtotal	515	
Insufficient data	35	
Total	550	

Case study 1

Pre-assessment

An elderly patient admitted for elective surgery was an asthmatic, hypertensive, morbidly obese with obstructive sleep apnoea dependant on nocturnal CPAP. The patient was seen in a pre-assessment clinic 10 days prior to their operation. Risks were discussed and a high dependency unit bed booked. Their spouse was fully briefed to bring the patients CPAP machine to the hospital. The patient underwent an uneventful operation under regional anaesthesia and was discharged within 24 hours of surgery.

The Advisors considered this demonstrated the benefit of timely pre-assessment.

Nutritional assessment

Only 28 patients had any record of a plan to improve their pre-operative nutritional status (Table 4.16). This finding was at odds with the organisational questionnaire which revealed that 81.8% of hospitals had nutritional policies.

Table 4.16 Documented nutritional plan

Documented nutritional plan	Number of patients	%
Yes	28	6.1
No	431	93.9
Subtotal	459	
Insufficient data	91	
Total	550	

Pre-operative malnutrition compromises surgical outcome while pre-operative nutritional impairment can lead to increased postoperative morbidity and mortality[26-28]. There is evidence to support the provision of nutritional support in severely malnourished patients prior to surgery. There are NICE guidelines indicating the need to identify and correct pre-operative nutritional impairment [29]. By contrast, enteral feeding positively influences gut barrier function, maintaining normal flora and mucosal immunity and is associated with a diminished acute phase response. However, in the group of patients reviewed routine pre-operative feeding was rare.

Of the 28 patients who had a nutritional plan in place it might have been expected that they would have been in a poor nutritional state with a low BMI. Table 4.17 shows the BMI ranges of the patients with a nutritional plan in place. Of note is that 21/28 were in the overweight categories with 10/28 being in the morbidly obese group. This suggests that although it is important for overweight patients to have nutritional plans in place it is disappointing that few malnourished (low BMI) patients were optimised nutritionally.

Table 4.17 Patients with a nutritional plan

BMI	Number of patients
< 16.5	0
16.5-18.49	1
18.5-24.99	3
25-29.99	7
30-34.99	2
35-39.99	2
≥ 40	10
Could not calculate BMI	3
Total	28

Case study 2

Nutritional assessment
A patient was admitted for an elective laryngectomy for carcinoma of the larynx. There was a history of dysphagia and the patient's weight was 50 Kg, height 1.7m with a BMI of 17.3.

The Advisors were surprised that this patient had no nutritional supplementation prior to operation.

Obesity is well known to have an effect on morbidity, resource utilisation and mortality. Given the high incidence of obesity in this study there are clearly opportunities to modify this risk factor in the elective patient group.

Pre-operative investigations
Table 4.18 shows that the Advisors considered that 55 patients had not had appropriate pre-operative investigations performed in elective patients.

Table 4.18 Necessary investigations performed

All necessary investigations were performed	Number of patients	%
Yes	343	86.2
No	55	13.8
Subtotal	398	
Not documented	45	
Insufficient data	107	
Total	550	

The Advisors judged that the investigations shown in Table 4.19 were omitted. Reasons for the omission of these tests were not identified. Standardised protocols for pre-operative assessment would reduce the omission of tests; equally these guidelines might also reduce the number of unnecessary investigations.

Table 4.19 Omitted investigations

Omitted Investigations	Number of patients
Urea & electrolytes	7
Full blood count	4
Blood gases	8
Chest X-ray	6
ECG	11
Echocardiography	10
Lung function tests	11
CPEX testing	6
Nutritional assessment	10

The Advisors considered that the standard of pre-operative assessment in elective patients was good or adequate 87% of patients (Table 4.20).

Table 4.20 Standard of pre-admission assessment

Pre-operative assessment clinic	Number of patients	%
Good	165	37.6
Adequate	217	49.4
Poor	51	11.6
Unacceptable	6	1.4
Subtotal	439	
Unable to assign grade	111	
Total	550	

However, the Advisors considered the standard of the assessment to be poor or unacceptable in 57 patients (13%).

Enhanced recovery programme

Enhanced recovery programmes are recent initiatives to improve patient outcomes and speed up recovery after surgery. The programme focuses on making sure that patients are active participants in their own recovery process. It also aims to ensure that patients always receive evidence based care at the right time.

Aims of the enhanced recovery programme are:
• Better outcomes and reduced length of stay;
• Increased numbers of patients being treated (if there is demand) or reduced level of resources necessary;
• Better staffing environment.

The elements of an enhanced recovery programme are:
• Pre-operative assessment, planning and preparation before admission;
• Reducing the physical stress of the operation;
• A structured approach to immediate post-operative and peri-operative management, including pain relief;
• Early mobilisation.

In only 19/550 elective patients was there any record of entrance into any form of enhanced recovery programme. Given the potential benefits of this type of approach enhanced recovery programmes for high risk patients should be adopted.

Pre-operative assessment for non-elective admissions

For those patients in the non-elective group 95.7% had a timely initial assessment (Table 4.21).

High risk non-elective patients may not be admitted directly to a surgical team and can present via a number of different referral pathways. The Advisors were of the opinion that non-elective patients who were admitted under an inpatient specialty, other than surgery, had a delayed referral to the correct surgical specialty in 16/85 (19%) cases.

Case study 3

Pre-operative assessment

A patient presented to a pre-assessment clinic prior to an elective total hip replacement. At the pre-assessment clinic it was noted that the patient had an abnormally high blood sugar and they were referred back to their GP for investigation of possible diabetes. The patient also had a history of angina and hypercholesterolaemia. Echocardiography showed aortic stenosis, mitral regurgitation, dilated left atrium and impaired left ventricular function. No action was taken by the GP and the patient presented on the day of operation with a BMI of 15.5. The anaesthetist made the decision to proceed and started an insulin sliding scale and arranged for a high dependency unit bed postoperatively. The patient's diabetes was initially hard to control in the postoperative period but soon became stable.

This case demonstrates the need for all parts of the patient care pathway to participate in optimisation if risk is to be reduced.

Table 4.21 Timely assessment of non-elective patients

Timely initial assessment	Number of patients	%
Yes	200	95.7
No	9	4.3
Subtotal	**209**	
Insufficient data	56	
Total	**265**	

Table 4.22 Evidence of a consultant review prior to surgery

Evidence of consultant surgeon review prior to surgery	Number of patients	%
Yes	105	49.8
No	27	12.8
Not documented	79	37.4
Subtotal	**211**	
Insufficient data	54	
Total	**265**	

A correct diagnosis is essential if outcome is to be optimal. Early senior clinical review should improve diagnostic accuracy in all clinical specialties. Working practices do not always facilitate the immediate presence of senior clinicians when non-elective patients are admitted. This is supported by the finding that there was evidence of non-elective patients being seen by consultants prior to surgery in only 50% of admissions (Table 4.22). However, the Advisors considered that the correct diagnosis had been reached in 233/240 (97%) patients.

Following review by a consultant surgeon the diagnosis changed in only 10 patients. The changed diagnoses included perforated sigmoid colon, adhesions causing small bowel obstruction, chronic chest problem, displaced intracapsular fracture of femur, fractured femur, cholelithiasis, cauda equina syndrome and pathological fracture.

Following diagnosis it is paramount that a management plan is devised.

The Advisors considered that 98.8% of patients had a management plan in place (Table 4.23).

Table 4.23 Management plan in place

Management plan	Number of patients	%
Yes	246	98.8
No	3	1.2
Subtotal	**249**	
Insufficient data	16	
Total	**265**	

The Advisors were asked whether the management plan consisted of further investigations, therapeutic interventions, senior review and a monitoring plan.

Of these 246 patients with management plans in place 183 indicated further investigations, 191 indicated therapeutic interventions, 144 indicated senior review and 97 indicated a monitoring plan. This appears to leave substantial gaps in a number of management plans. Of note is the lack of a monitoring plan, which is an essential component of recognising patient deterioration in a timely manner.

The management plan was considered by the Advisors to be satisfactory in 200 cases but unsatisfactory in 33 cases (14%). The remainder (13 cases) could not be assessed. Following consultant review the management plan changed in 29 cases.

Delay in implementation of a management plan may result if appropriate investigations are not carried out. The Advisors were of the opinion that appropriate investigations had been performed in 227/235 (96.6%) patients (Table 4.24).

Table 4.24 Appropriateness of surgical investigations

Appropriate surgical investigations	Number of patients	%
Yes	227	96.6
No	8	3.4
Subtotal	235	
Insufficient data	30	
Total	265	

Those investigations considered to be missing included:- arterial blood gases, echocardiogram, CT scan of head, CT of abdomen, chest X-ray, ECG, urinanalysis, septic screen and "blood test".

The Advisors believed that there were delays in obtaining surgical investigations in 18/213 (8.5%) patients (Table 4.25). Non-elective patients need to be investigated in a timely manner, any delay in the correct treatment may affect outcome. Case study 4 shows an example of this.

Case study 4

Delay due to unnecessary test

An elderly patient fell and sustained a fractured neck of femur. The patient had a history of rheumatoid arthritis, hypertension, chronic renal impairment and abnormal cholinesterase. Their exercise tolerance was one mile on the flat. The patient had no cardiac symptoms and had had a regional anaesthetic for another operation six months previously. An anaesthetic registrar saw the patient on the day of admission and noted a soft systolic murmur. There were no signs of left ventricular hypertrophy on chest X-ray or ECG. The registrar ordered an echocardiogram which delayed the patient's operation by 24 hours.

The Advisors were of the opinion that the registrar should have sought senior advice as the cardiac investigation was probably unnecessary and it delayed the treatment. On this occasion it was felt that it did not affect outcome but it is well recognised in this group of patients that outcome is dependent on early surgery.

Table 4.25 Delay in obtaining investigations

Delay in obtaining surgical investigations	Number of patients	%
Yes	18	8.5
No	195	91.5
Subtotal	213	
Insufficient data	52	
Total	265	

Comorbidities

As already stated, comorbidities were frequent in the whole prospective data set but the incidence was much higher in the peer reviewed group (1203 comorbidities in 829 peer reviewed patients [1.5 comorbidities per patient] compared with 10846 comorbidities in 19372 patients [0.6 comorbidities per patient])

Within the non-elective peer reviewed group, 91.1% had comorbidities identified (Table 4.26) and 40.1% had a recorded plan to optimise these comorbidities (Table 4.27).

Table 4.26 Comorbidities in the non-elective group

Comorbidities	Number of patients	%
Yes	235	91.1
No	23	8.9
Subtotal	258	
Insufficient data	7	
Total	265	

Table 4.27 Evidence of a plan to optimise comorbidities in the non-elective group

Plan to optimise	Number of patients	%
Yes	91	40.1
No	136	59.9
Subtotal	227	
Insufficient data	8	
Total	235	

Many patients may have had their comorbidities recognised and considered but because of time constraints, surgery was expedited. The optimisation of comorbidities improves outcome. Clinicians should formally document plans with regard to the peri-operative management of comorbidities. Standard operating policies for the peri-operative management of comorbidities would assist in ensuring the optimisation of pre-existing comorbidities.

The Advisors graded the standard pre-operative assessment in non-elective patients as good or adequate in 90.1% of patients and poor or unacceptable in 9.9% (Table 4.28).

Table 4.28 Standard of pre-operative assessment of non-elective patients

Pre-operative assessment	Number of patients	%
Good	86	38.7
Adequate	114	51.4
Poor	20	9.0
Unacceptable	2	<1
Subtotal	222	
Unable to assign grade	43	
Total	265	

4.6 Consent

A proper consent process is essential to ensure that patients understand treatment options and the alternatives together with the risks, benefits and likely outcomes of any proposed treatment. In this group of high risk patients with a likely substantial burden of morbidity and mortality one would think that clinicians would place a greater emphasis on the importance of good consent.

As part of the peer review process we requested that the consent form for the operative procedure was provided to NCEPOD for review by the Advisors. This was provided in 512/829 cases (62%).

The grade of doctor who signed the consent form is shown in Table 4.29.

Table 4.29 Grade of doctor signing the consent form

Grade	Number of patients	%
Consultant	140	42.0
Clinical Fellow	5	1.5
Staff Grade or Associate Specialist	28	8.4
Trainee with CCT	2	<1
Senior specialist trainee (SpR1+ or ST3+)	126	37.8
Junior specialist trainee (ST1 & ST2 or CTs)	32	9.6
Subtotal	**333**	
Not documented	179	
Total	**512**	

The Advisors were asked to consider if consent had been obtained by the correct grade of doctor. In 113 cases they could come to no judgment. However in 345 cases they felt the grade of doctor was appropriate and in 54 cases (14%) not appropriate (Table 4.30).

Table 4.30 Grade of doctor signing the consent appropriate – Advisors' view

Appropriate grade	Number of patients	%
Yes	345	86.5
No	54	13.5
Subtotal	**399**	
Not documented	113	
Total	**512**	

Advisors were also asked if they considered the consent process to be adequate. This opinion was made with reference to the consent form and information available in the medical notes, but was only made in cases where the consent form had actually been returned to NCEPOD.

Table 4.31 shows the Advisors opinion of adequacy of consent. In 116 cases (23%) they did not feel that this was so.

Table 4.31 Advisors' opinions on the adequacy of the consent taken

Adequate consent	Number of patients	%
Yes	386	77.0
No	116	23.0
Subtotal	**502**	
Not documented	10	
Total	**512**	

The Advisors were of the opinion that 33/512 patients were not competent to give informed consent. 25 of these 33 had evidence of the correct consent pathway being followed for patients who lack competence to give consent. However, Case study 5 demonstrates a good example of consent taking.

As this population of patients was considered high risk it might be expected that mortality estimates would be found on the consent form. Table 4.32 shows that this was only found in 37/496 cases.

Table 4.32 Mortality risk documented on the consent form

Mortality risk on consent form	Number of patients	%
Yes	37	7.5
No	459	92.5
Subtotal	**496**	
Not answered	16	
Total	**512**	

Case study 5

Consent

A very elderly patient was admitted from a nursing home for a hysteroscopy, cystoscopy and biopsy. The patient had a mini mental score of 3/10. The need for operation was discussed with the manager of their care home and next of kin and consent form 4 was used to document this process.

The Advisors felt that this demonstrated good practice with respect to consent for surgery.

Documentation of risk in the medical notes

Risks can also be documented in the medical notes so the Advisors were asked to assess if this route had been used to document mortality risk where it had not been documented on the consent form. Additional information on mortality risk was only found in seven sets of medical records. In total, in only 45/644 (7%) of cases was there any record of the risk of mortality. Case study 6 shows an example of this.

The General Medical Council (GMC) requires that doctors must have effective discussions with patients about risk[30]. Doctors must identify the adverse outcomes that may result from the proposed options. This includes the potential outcome of taking no action. Risks can take a number of forms, but will usually be side effects, complications and failure of an intervention to achieve the desired aim.

Risks can vary from common but minor side effects, to rare but serious adverse outcomes possibly resulting in permanent disability or death.

The GMC requires that doctors inform patients if an investigation or treatment might result in a serious adverse outcome, even if the likelihood is very small.

For each patient the mortality risk and the risk of morbidity should be defined, documented and made explicit to the patient and all involved in the patient's peri-operative journey. This might inform the standards of care throughout the patient's hospital episode.

The NHS and independent organisations such as the Dr Foster database collect outcome data and individual clinicians should know their individual mortality and morbidity figures.

Case study 6

Documentation of risk

A blind and deaf resident of a nursing home sustained a fractured neck of femur following a fall. They were known to have a history of dementia and Parkinson's disease. It was noted that the patient would need a consent form 4 on admission. Throughout their admission the patient's relatives were kept informed and consulted. However, there was no documented risk during the consent process.

The Advisors considered that in this patient risk should have been discussed and documented.

4.7 Pre-operative phase

This section looks at the care of patients in the period after admission and initial assessment until commencement of surgery.

As previously shown comorbidities were very common, as one would expect in a high risk sample. At least one comorbidity was present in 752/808 (93%) patients.

Many patients who die within 30 days of surgery do so in general wards. Of these, many have significant comorbidities such as co-existing cardiovascular or respiratory disease. It has been reported that about 42% of patients who died following surgery had pre-operative assessment scores recorded as ASA (American Society of Anesthesiologists Score) of 3 or less which suggests that the severity of the illness and actual risk of death was not fully appreciated in the pre-operative assessment. Previously it has been reported that subjective assessment underestimated the risk of death for patients undergoing surgery[31].

Advisors were asked, in their opinion, if comorbidities, where present, were recognised. Table 4.33 shows that they were recognised in 94% of cases.

Table 4.33 All comorbidities recognised

All comorbidities recognised	Number of patients	%
Yes	648	93.6
No	44	6.4
Subtotal	692	
Insufficient data	60	
Total	752	

Recognition of comorbidities provides the opportunity to intervene and optimise the patient's condition pre-operatively. Table 4.34 below shows that in only 29% of patients who had comorbidities was there a documented plan to optimise these conditions prior to surgery.

Table 4.34 Documented plan to optimise comorbidities

Documented plan to optimise	Number of patients	%
Yes	199	28.6
No	497	71.4
Subtotal	696	
Insufficient data	56	
Total	752	

The opportunity to intervene will be affected by the urgency of surgery. In this respect it should be noted that 590 patients were classified as elective (439) or expedited (127) (Table 4.4) and that the opportunity for intervention should have been present. It would appear that there is a missed opportunity to prepare high risk patients for surgery and potentially improve outcomes.

Case study 7

Pre-operative optimisation
The patient presented with a large femoral hernia had a history of hypertension, previous stroke, atrial fibrillation, COPD, osteoarthritis and deafness. On admission their INR was 5.0. Surgery was postponed awaiting a normalisation of the INR. In the two days prior to surgery the patient was reviewed by an orthogeriatrician on two occasions prior to surgery in order to optimise their medical state. The patient was also seen promptly by a critical care outreach team when they became temporarily tachypnoeic.

The Advisors considered this to be a good example of both recognition of a high risk patient and the pre-operative management with a view to optimisation.

It has long been recognised that routine pre-operative optimisation of patients undergoing major elective surgery would be a significant and cost effective improvement in peri-operative care[32].

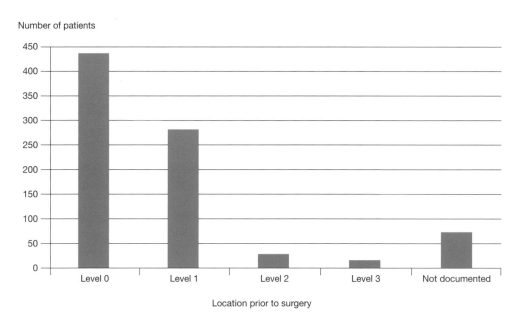

Number of patients

Figure 4.4 Location of patients prior to surgery

Location of patients prior to surgery

The location of a patient prior to surgery will affect an organisation's ability to optimise the patient's condition. Figure 4.4 shows the location of patients prior to surgery. 58% were situated in a level 0 ward bed, 37% level 1, 3% level 2 and 2% level 3.

In the opinion of the Advisors this was the correct location in 707/749 patients (Table 4.35).

Table 4.35 Appropriateness of the patients' location prior to surgery – Advisors' opinion

Correct location	Number of patients	%
Yes	707	94.4
No	42	5.6
Subtotal	749	
Insufficient data	14	
Total	763	

When asked where the 42 patients they considered not to be in the correct pre-operative location should have been the Advisors considered that 25 should have been in level 2 care, 11 in level 1 care and 4 level 0 (Table 4.36).

Table 4.36 Where patients should have gone prior to surgery – Advisors' opinion

Type of ward	Number of patients
Level 0	4
Level 1	11
Level 2	25
Subtotal	40
Not answered	2
Total	42

From the case note extracts 39 patients went to level 2 or 3 care areas prior to surgery. Thirteen patients were admitted for the stabilisation of an acute physiological disturbance and 4 for pre-operative optimisation, 22 had no documented reason. Of the 39 patients who were in a critical care unit pre-operatively, 20 were elective cases and 19 non-elective cases.

Pre-operative fluid optimisation

The optimisation of pre-operative intravascular fluid volume minimises morbidity and mortality, but the practical delivery of such care remains a challenge. Estimates of fluid depletion remain inaccurate and may lead to inappropriate replacement. Physiological compensatory mechanisms can mask hypovolaemia. Optimisation of peri-operative volume status has been shown to improve outcome. The GIFTASUP guidelines state "In high risk surgical patients pre-operative treatment with intravenous fluid and inotropes should be aimed at achieving predetermined goals for cardiac output and oxygen delivery" in order to improve outcome"[33].

The Advisors considered that in 502/535 patients, pre-operative fluid management was adequate. In this group of patients the 30 day mortality was 5% (Table 4.37). In the group of patients in whom fluid management was considered to be inadequate the mortality was 20% and in those in whom it was excessive 33%.

When examining the entire cohort of patients with regard to where they were prior to surgery and the adequacy of fluid management. The adequacy of fluid management was better in higher care level areas than on the general wards (Table 4.38).

Table 4.37 Adequacy of pre-operative fluid management and mortality

Pre-operative fluid management	30 day mortality			
	Alive	Deceased	% mortality	Total
Adequate	502	25	4.7	527
Inadequate	31	8	20.5	39
Excessive	2	1	33.3	3
Subtotal	535	34	6.0	569
Insufficient data	237	23	8.8	260
Total	772	57	6.9	829

Table 4.38 Adequacy of pre-operative fluid management by ward type

Pre-operative ward	Pre-operative fluid management					
	Adequate	Inadequate	Excessive	Subtotal	Insufficient data	Total
Level 0 or 1	479	37	3	519	207	726
Level 2 or 3	25	1		26	13	39
Subtotal	504	38	3	545	220	765
Not documented	23	1	0	24	40	64
Total	527	39	3	569	260	829

Pre-operative fluids were given to 30% of the patients in the peer review group overall (Table 4.39).

Table 4.39 Administration of pre-operative fluids

IV fluids	Number of patients	%
Yes	209	28.8
No	517	71.2
Subtotal	726	
Insufficient data	103	
Total	829	

When the group was split into elective and non-elective patients 10% of elective patients were given fluids and 70% of non-elective patients (Table 4.40). This would reflect the urgent nature of non-elective surgery and the acute conditions that necessitate non elective surgery.

The Advisors found that there was evidence of pre-operative hypovolaemia in 36/650 patients (Table 4.41). In this group the mortality at 30 days was 31% compared to a mortality of 5.4% in the group in whom the Advisors considered there to have been no pre-operative hypovolaemia. The need to resuscitate patients adequately prior to surgery is well recognised as confirmed by this data.

Table 4.40 Type of surgery and pre-operative intra venous fluids

Type of surgery	IV fluids pre-operatively			Subtotal	Insufficient data	Total
	Yes	No	% given fluids			
Elective	47	439	9.7	486	64	550
Non elective	159	72	68.8	231	34	265
Subtotal	206	511	28.7	717	98	815
Not answered	3	4	42.9	7	7	14
Total	209	515	28.9	724	105	829

Table 4.41 Pre-operative hypovolaemia and mortality

Evidence of pre-operative hypovolaemia	30 day mortality			Total
	Alive	Deceased	% mortality	
Yes	36	16	30.8	52
No	614	35	5.4	649
Subtotal	650	51	7.3	701
Insufficient data	121	7	5.5	128
Total	771	58	7.0	829

The 52 patients considered to be hypovolaemic were in both elective and non elective groups Table 4.42.

Table 4.42 Hypovolaemic patients

Admission category	Number of patients
Non-elective	43
Elective	7
Subtotal	**50**
Insufficient data	2
Total	**52**

In the 52 patients with evidence of hypovolaemia the Advisors considered the pre-operative fluid management to have been adequate in 28/40 patients and inadequate or excessive in 11/40 patients (Table 4.43)

Table 4.43 Adequacy of fluid management and hypovolaemia

Pre-operative fluid management	Number of patients
Adequate	28
Inadequate	11
Excessive	1
Subtotal	**40**
Insufficient data	12
Total	**52**

In those patients in whom the Advisors considered fluid management to be inadequate six had had no intravenous fluids administered pre-operatively (Table 4.44).

Table 4.44 Fluid administration in patients with inadequate fluid therapy

IV fluids	Number of patients	%
Yes	43	87.8
No	6	12.2
Subtotal	**49**	
Insufficient data	3	
Total	**52**	

The 30 day mortality in those hypovolaemic patients in whom the Advisors considered there to have been inadequate pre-operative fluid management was 55% compared to 21% mortality in those with adequate pre-operative fluid therapy (Table 4.45). This reinforces previous evidence outlining the beneficial effects on outcome of optimisation of fluid status prior to surgery.

The adequate delivery of fluid management and optimisation may well be beyond the resources available on a general ward. When the adequacy of fluid management against pre-operative location was examined, those who where in a higher level of care universally had adequate fluid therapy (Table 4.46). This highlights the known advantages of optimising patients in higher care level areas prior to high risk surgery.

Table 4.45 Pre-operative fluid management by mortality

Pre-operative fluid management	Alive	Deceased	% mortality	Total
Adequate	22	6	21.4	28
Inadequate	5	6	54.5	11
Excessive	1	0	0.0	1
Subtotal	**28**	**12**	**30.0**	**40**
Insufficient data	8	4	33.3	12
Total	**36**	**16**	**30.8**	**52**

Table 4.46 Pre-operative site and adequacy of fluid management

Pre-operative ward	Pre-operative fluid management			Subtotal	Insufficient data	Total
	Adequate	Inadequate	Excessive			
Level 0 or 1	20	11	1	32	8	40
Level 2 or 3	7	0	0	7	3	10
Subtotal	27	11	1	39	11	50
Not documented	1	0	0	1	1	2
Total	28	11	1	40	12	52

Case study 8

Pre-operative fluid optimisation

A patient with a history of hypertension, ischaemic heart disease and diverticulitis was admitted with a 24 hour history of severe abdominal pain. On admission their pulse was 100bpm, blood pressure 90/60 and urine output had fallen to 10 mls/hour. Capillary refill was recorded as 7 seconds. A CT scan of their abdomen suggested that they had a perforated viscous and a decision was made to take the patient to theatre for a laparotomy. Prior to surgery the patient was admitted to a high dependency unit where an arterial line and central venous catheter were inserted and their cardiovascular system optimised. Prior to going to theatre the patient's observations were temperature 36°C, pulse 78 bpm, blood pressure 110/78 and 70 mls of urine had been passed in the previous hour.

The Advisors considered this to be good care and resuscitation of a hypovolaemic patient in the pre-operative period.

High risk patients should have fluid optimisation in a higher care level area if it is to be adequate and contribute to better outcomes.

A small group of patients had bowel preparation pre-operatively. However only 4/22 of these patients received intravenous fluids pre-operatively.

As reported, pre-operative hypovolaemia carries an increase in mortality and morbidity. Bowel preparation has been shown to cause severe side-effects such as electrolyte or acid-base imbalances and dehydration. Unregulated fluid infusion, to re-establish the reduced intravascular volume, may worsen the physiological stress response to surgery. This approach has been found to prolong wound healing and bowel function recovery time and increase reintervention rate, hospital stay, mortality, and the incidence of severe cardiopulmonary complications. The necessity of pre-operative bowel preparation is now under scrutiny[34]. Patients receiving bowel preparation require well monitored fluid therapy.

4.8 Intra-operative phase

Timing of surgery

When asked if the patients received timely surgery, there was a difference between the elective and non-elective groups. Whilst only 2% of elective patients failed to receive appropriately timed surgery, 20% of non-elective patients failed to receive timely surgery (Table 4.47).

Table 4.47 Timely surgery

Surgery timely once decision made	Elective	%	Non-elective	%
Yes	476	98	196	80
No	11	2	49	20
Subtotal	487		245	
Insufficient data	63		20	
Total	550		265	

The 60 patients who were in the delayed surgery group were given the following reasons for delay: Lack of surgeon (6); Lack of anaesthetist (3) and Lack of theatre space (28). The delay in surgery was considered to have affected outcome in nine patients.

Resources have been concentrated on elective patients for many years and the lack of access for emergency/ urgent patients has been a focus of previous NCEPOD reports. Daytime, staffed and available operating theatres (CEPOD theatres) had increased in availability over the years: 'Who Operates When 1997' (51%), 'Who Operates When II 2003' (63%), 'Caring to the End 2009' (87%) and it is particularly disappointing to see that 'CEPOD' theatre availability has dropped to 72.5% in this study (p15 Table 2.1). Delay in operating on non-elective patients is unacceptable.

Grade of surgeon

The Advisors considered that in only four patients was the grade of surgeon inappropriate for the complexity of the surgery (Table 4.48).

Table 4.48 Appropriate grade of surgeon – Advisors' opinion

Grade of surgeon appropriate	Number of patients	%
Yes	373	98.9
No	4	1.1
Subtotal	377	
Insufficient data	31	
Total	408	

Note this could not be answered for 421 patients as the grade of surgeon was not documented.

The majority of high risk patients are being operated on by the correct grade of surgeon.

Grade of anaesthetist

The Advisors were of the opinion when reviewing the case notes that 14 patients were anaesthetised by an inappropriate grade of anaesthetist (Table 4.49). This represents a four fold increase in inappropriate care with regard to anaesthesia when compared with surgery. High risk patients must be cared for by clinicians of appropriate seniority.

Table 4.49 Grade of anaesthetist appropriate

Grade of anaesthetist appropriate	Number of patients	%
Yes	283	95.3
No	14	4.7
Subtotal	297	
Grade not documented	295	
Insufficient data	237	
Total	829	

Intra-operative complications

Intra-operative complications were identified in 9.8% of patients. Patients who suffer intra-operative complications had a 30 day mortality of 13.2 % compared to 5.7% in those without (Table 4.50).

Table 4.50 Intra-operative complications by outcome

Intra-operative complications	Alive	Deceased	% mortality
No	662	40	5.7
Yes	66	10	13.2
Subtotal	728	50	6.4
Insufficient data	44	7	13.7
Total	772	57	6.9

Monitoring

The adequate monitoring of patients allows for the early identification of changes in their condition. Physiological monitoring is essential during high risk surgery and anaesthesia, if deterioration and complications are to be avoided. The Advisors considered intra-operative monitoring was inadequate in 10.6% of patients (Table 4.51).

Table 4.51 Adequate monitoring

Adequate monitoring	Number of patients	%
Yes	644	89.4
No	76	10.6
Subtotal	720	
Insufficient data	109	
Total	829	

The group who had inadequate monitoring, in the Advisors' opinion, had a threefold increase in mortality, supporting the essential requirement for high risk patients to be fully monitored throughout the operative period (Table 4.52).

Table 4.52 Adequate monitoring by outcome

Adequate monitoring	Alive	Deceased	% mortality
Yes	607	37	5.7
No	64	12	15.8
Subtotal	671	49	6.8
Insufficient data	101	8	7.3
Total	772	57	6.9

The Advisors considered that an arterial line for intra-operative monitoring was the most often required but not used technique.

Only 6/491 patients had any form of blood flow/cardiac output monitoring. Advisors were of the opinion that cardiac output monitoring would have been appropriate in a further 77/655 (12%) patients.

Fluid management

Haemodynamic optimisation (accurate fluid intervention) guided by a cardiac output algorithm can significantly reduce rates of complications and mortality and significantly reduces length of hospital stay. Similarly, patient warming during surgery, beta blockade, higher supplemental inspired oxygen and optimised administration of blood products also show benefit Intra-operative fluid management affects outcome. The Advisors considered fluid management to be adequate in 91.6% of patients (Table 4.53).

Table 4.53 Adequacy of fluid management

Intra-operative fluid management	Number of patients	%
Adequate	610	91.6
Inadequate	38	5.7
Excessive	18	2.7
Subtotal	666	
Insufficient data	163	
Total	829	

Table 4.54 GIFTASUP guidelines used

Fluid therapy within GIFTASUP guidelines	Number of patients	%
Yes	496	87.0
No	74	13.0
Subtotal	570	
Type of fluid therapy not documented	69	
Insufficient data	190	
Total	829	

The Advisors identified that in 74 patients fluid therapy fell outside the GIFTASUP guidelines (Table 4.54). The GIFTASUP guidelines were developed [33] as concern had arisen as a result of identification of a high incidence of postoperative sodium and water overload, and evidence

Table 4.55 Vaso-active drugs used

Drugs used	Adrenaline	Noradrenaline	Dobutamine	Dopexamine
Yes	9	27	4	9
No	715	690	716	704
Subtotal	724	717	720	713
Insufficient data	105	112	109	116
Total	829	829	829	829

to suggest that preventing or treating this, by more accurate fluid therapy, would improve outcome.

The reasons why patients fell outside the GIFTASUP guidelines were in broad categories and included poor monitoring, particularly of cardiac output and the use of normal saline.

Vaso-active agents
The use of vaso-active agents intra-operatively appeared to be associated with a higher mortality. The 30 day mortality was 21.6% in the 37 patients who received intra-operative vaso-active agents, the details of type used is shown in Table 4.55.

Quality of the anaesthetic record
The Advisors considered that the anaesthetic note was poor or unacceptable in 9.7% of patients (Table 4.56). The Advisors frequently commented on a failure to record, times, dates, grades and supervising consultants to name but a few.

Table 4.56 Quality of the anaesthetic record

Quality of anaesthetic note	Number of patients	%
Good	319	46.9
Adequate	295	43.4
Poor	57	8.4
Unacceptable	9	1.3
Subtotal	680	
Insufficient data	149	
Total	829	

Intra-operative care in summary
The Advisors considered that the overall intra-operative care was good or adequate in 97.4% of patients and poor or unacceptable in 2.6% (Table 4.57).

Table 4.57 Standard of intra-operative care

Standard of intra-operative care	Number of patients	%
Good	380	53.4
Adequate	313	44.0
Poor	16	2.3
Unacceptable	2	<1
Subtotal	711	
Insufficient data	118	
Total	829	

4.9 Postoperative phase

The standard of postoperative care that is delivered to patients will be determined by a combination of factors e.g. availability of facilities, availability of staff, perception of risk of adverse outcomes and acceptance of current care pathways. In the introduction it was highlighted that the UK has a lower proportion of critical care beds than comparable countries. The different level of availability of critical care resources has produced a care pathway where a low percentage of patients have access to critical care. This is such an ingrained practice in the UK that it has become the accepted dogma.

Postoperative location

The first care location for many patients after surgery has finished is a post anaesthetic recovery area (PACU). In the organisation section it was shown that 289/293 hospitals (99%) had a post-anaesthetic recovery area and in 192/287 hospitals (67%) this was available continuously (24 hours per day, 7 days per week). Within the peer review group of patients 679/829 were documented to have spent time in a recovery area.

Table 4.58 shows discharge destination for patients who did not spend time in recovery.

Table 4.58 Destination if not recovery

Postoperative ward	Number of patients
Level 0	2
Level 1	1
Level 2	23
Level 3	40
Insufficient data	3
Total	69

As expected this was almost entirely accounted for by patients who were admitted directly to critical care from theatre and is not a practice of concern.

The post-anaesthetic recovery area should be staffed and have the appropriate skilled personnel to ensure that the patient is suitably recovered from surgery and sufficiently stable to be safely cared for after discharge.

The Advisors' opinion of whether the patient was stable and fit for discharge from recovery is shown in Table 4.59.

Table 4.59 Patient stable and fit for discharge – Advisors' opinion

Patient stable in PACU	Number of patients	%
Yes	564	95.3
No	28	4.7
Subtotal	592	
Insufficient data	87	
Total	679	

As can be seen the Advisors considered that 95% of patients were fit to be discharged from the post anaesthetic care area and had concerns in 28 cases. Of these 28 patients 4 were dead at 30 days. This represents a 14% 30 day mortality rate this reinforces the concerns raised in the prospective data analysis where there was an increased mortality in patients overall (both low and high risk) when clinicians raised concerns over the discharge of patients from postoperative recovery areas.

There are some objective markers of fitness for discharge to the ward. One of these is normothermia as it is well known that inadvertent peri-operative hypothermia has adverse physiological consequences and is associated with poor outcomes. NICE clinical guidance 65 provides more detail and recommendations regarding avoidance of peri-operative hypothermia[21]. Table 4.60 shows the last recorded temperature before discharge from recovery.

Table 4.60 Last recorded temperature before discharge

Temperature °C	Number of patients	%
≥36.0	360	87.2
<36.0	53	12.8
Subtotal	413	
Not documented	266	
Total	679	

As can be seen 53/413 patients whose temperature was documented were hypothermic and in 266/679 (39%) it did not appear that temperature had been documented. NICE CG 65 states that patients should not be transferred from recovery until temperature is 36°C or greater.

Tables 4.61 and 4.62 show the last recorded pulse and respiratory rate before discharge from recovery.

Table 4.61 Last recorded pulse before discharge

Pulse	Number of patients	%
≤50	29	5.2
51-60	79	14.1
61-100	425	76.0
101-110	18	3.2
≥111	8	1.4
Subtotal	559	
Not documented	120	
Total	679	

Table 4.62 Last recorded respiratory rate before discharge

Respiratory rate	Number of patients	%
<12	26	5.0
12-16	380	75.4
17-20	90	17.4
>20	22	4.2
Subtotal	518	
Not documented	161	
Total	679	

As can been seen the majority of patients have physiological parameters within an acceptable range. However, the number of patients with documented low and high pulse rates and respiratory rates on discharge from recovery is of concern. In addition the lack of documentation of these parameters in a substantial number of cases is not in keeping with good practice. Discharge criteria should be adhered to and escalation policies in place if these criteria are not met.

Table 4.63 shows the patient location that the patients were discharged to from the recovery area (or directly from theatre if they bypassed a recovery area).

Table 4.63 Area to which patients were discharged after recovery

Type of ward	Number of patients	%
Level 0	330	41.9
Level 1	278	35.3
Level 2	129	16.4
Level 3	50	6.4
Subtotal	787	
Not documented	14	
Insufficient data	28	
Total	829	

One hundred and twenty nine patients went to level 2 care and 50 patients went to level 3 care. This represents 23% of the peer reviewed group (the corresponding figure for all the high risk patients in the prospective data set was also 23% (529/2321)).

Table 4.64 Outcome at 30 days post operation by level of ward care

Type of ward	Alive	Deceased	% mortality	Total
Level 0	315	15	4.5	330
Level 1	262	17	6.1	278
Level 2	117	11	8.5	129
Level 3	38	12	24.0	50
Total	732	55	7.0	787

Mortality related to discharge location

Table 4.64 shows the 30 day mortality related to location following discharge from recovery. As would be expected the mortality increases with increasing level of care as the sickest patients would be expected to receive the higher levels of care postoperatively.

The Advisors were asked to consider if the patient was discharge from recovery (or directly from theatre if they bypassed a recovery area) to the correct location (Table 4.65).

Table 4.65 Correct postoperative location – Advisors' opinion

Correct postoperative location	Number of patients	%
Yes	703	91.7
No	64	8.3
Subtotal	767	
Insufficient data	20	
Total	787	

When looking at the 30 day outcome of those patients considered not to have been discharged to the correct area we find that this group has a three fold increase in 30 day mortality. This provides support for more routine critical care for high risk patients undergoing surgery. Table 4.66 shows outcome related to correct postoperative location.

In the majority of cases the Advisors stated that the discharge location was appropriate although there were concerns in 65 cases (8%) This appears relatively reassuring but must be set in the context of what the literature tells us and this study supports: many high risk patients do not access critical care, most postoperative deaths are in the high risk population, patients who develop complications and have late admission to critical care have poorer outcomes than those admitted initially and many postoperative patients who die do so without ever accessing critical care. Is it possible that clinicians have become so accepting of the lack of availability of critical care support for high risk surgical patients who it is not considered to be undesirable practice?

Table 4.66 Outcome at 30 days post operation compared with correct postoperative location

Correct location postoperatively	Alive	Deceased	% mortality	Total
Yes	660	42	6.0	702
No	52	13	20.0	65
Subtotal	712	55	7.2	767
Insufficient data	20	0	0.0	20
Total	732	55	7.0	787

Case study 9

Postoperative location

A patient was admitted with a complex humeral head fracture and was known to have hypertension, osteoporosis, pernicious anaemia, diverticulitis, be hypothyroid and have a reduced exercise tolerance. An echocardiogram showed aortic stenosis with a mean gradient of 30 mmHg, mitral valve regurgitation, tricuspid regurgitation and a dilated right atrium. The left ventricle showed mild impairment. Following operation the patient returned to the ward. For some days they remained unstable.

The Advisors considered that the unstable postoperative period might have been avoided had this patient been transferred to a higher care level area postoperatively.

Case study 10

Postoperative care

A patient was admitted from a surgical clinic following an incidental finding of a 7cm abdominal aortic aneurysm. They patient was on aspirin for a previous TIA and had type II diabetes. They underwent uneventful open surgery four days later and returned directly to the general ward post-operatively. There were analgesia problems in the immediate postoperative period. The patient was discharged home on day six.

The Advisors considered that this patient might have had a smoother postoperative course and shorter hospital stay, had they been admitted to a higher care level area postoperatively.

Use of early warning scores

For those patients not discharged to a higher care level area, only 360/489 (74%) had records of being in an early warning scoring system or 'track and trigger' system for the detection of a deterioration in their physiological status. This is not in keeping with NICE CG 50 'Acutely ill patients in hospital. Recognition of and response to acute illness in adults in hospital'[18] and raises concerns that in a quarter of high risk patients returned to ward care there may be scope for delays in recognising any clinical deterioration (Table 4.67).

Table 4.67 Early warning system used

Early warning system	Number of patients	%
Yes	360	73.6
No	129	26.4
Subtotal	489	
Insufficient data	119	
Total	608	

In only 21 patients of the 608 who were not admitted to a critical care area was there evidence of referral to, or involvement of, a critical care outreach team. Of these referrals, five were a planned review and 14 a review in response to clinical deterioration and concerns.

Of the 608 patients who were discharged from theatre to a ward (level 0 or 1) immediately after theatre, 26 patients (4%) were later admitted to a critical care area. In total 33 patients were identified as having been referred to critical care for an escalation of care. The Advisors considered that a further 37 patients should have been referred to critical care and they considered that in 20 of these 37 patients critical care admission would have affected outcome. This suggests that deterioration in a patient's condition was not being identified and referral for a higher level of care not expedited to attempt to reverse this deterioration. The failure to identify and treat a physiological deterioration in sick patients is a theme that runs through many NCEPOD reports.

Abnormal biochemical or haematological findings can give an indication of deterioration or development of complications. Tables 4.68 and 4.69 show the number of patients in whom biochemistry or haematology tests were requested. These data show that one in four high risk patients do not have blood parameters monitored and therefore may be at risk of postoperative deterioration going unnoticed.

Table 4.68 Biochemistry ordered

Biochemistry ordered	Number of patients	%
Yes	422	60.4
No	172	24.6
Not documented	105	15.0
Subtotal	699	
Insufficient data	130	
Total	829	

Table 4.69 Haematology ordered

Haematology ordered	Number of patients	%
Yes	446	64.0
No	161	23.1
Not documented	90	12.9
Subtotal	697	
Insufficient data	132	
Total	829	

One hundred and twenty seven of the patients received postoperative blood transfusions. It appears that 1 in 8 high risk patients received blood transfusions (Table 4.70).

Table 4.70 Blood transfusion received

Received transfusion	Number of patients	%
Yes	127	16.8
No	628	83.2
Subtotal	755	
Insufficient data	74	
Total	829	

With 91/127 patients (71%) receiving only one or two units of blood.

The Advisors considered that adequate analgesia was given in 629/829 patients. Non-steroidal anti inflammatory drugs (NSAIDs) were used as part of the analgesic regimen in 156 patients (Table 4.71).

Table 4.71 NSAIDs used

NSAIDs used	Number of patients	%
Yes	156	22.2
No	545	77.8
Subtotal	701	
Insufficient data	128	
Total	829	

In 21/156 cases where NSAIDs were used the Advisors considered that it was unsafe to have used this class of drug. Most of the concerns were around renal function and presence of hypovolaemia. NCEPOD has previously highlighted the contribution of NSAIDs to avoidable and preventable renal injury[35].

Prophylaxis against deep venous thrombosis was given to 572/829 patients and in 499 of these patients the therapy was within NICE guidelines.

Table 4.72 Postoperative complications

Postoperative complications	Number of patients	% of sample
Respiratory	82	9.9
Cardiovascular	70	8.4
Hospital acquired infection	53	6.4
Bleeding/haematoma	52	6.3
Renal	45	5.4
Metabolic	37	4.5
Neurological	28	3.4
Deep vein thrombosis	7	<1
Pulmonary embolism	3	<1

Postoperative complications were common and 377 separate complications were noted (Table 4.72). Whilst some patients developed multiple complications it can be appreciated that many of these high risk patients did not have a smooth postoperative pathway. Respiratory and cardiovascular complications were the most common.

Case study 11

Postoperative complications
A patient with chronic renal failure and a previous stroke underwent an elective total knee replacement. In the postoperative peri-operative fluid balance was not managed well. The patient went into congestive cardiac failure and required admission to level 2 intensive care. Their fluid status was optimised over a 48 hour period and the patient returned to the general ward.

This case highlights the need to accurately manage fluid balance in high risk surgical patients postoperatively.

If we look more closely at those patients who suffered gastrointestinal complications postoperatively they numbered 59 (7.8%) (Table 4.73).

Table 4.73 Gastrointestinal complications

Evidence of gastrointestinal complications	Number of patients	%
Yes	59	7.8
No	698	92.2
Subtotal	757	
Insufficient data	72	
Total	829	

In the group of 59 identified as having had gastrointestinal (GI) complications 20 had a prolonged ileus, six had a GI perforation, 11 had a GI bleed and 7 had an anastamotic leak.

Complications contribute to a poor patient experience, poor outcomes and higher resource utilisation. In one study[36] complications had a greater impact on outcome then pre or intra-operative factors. Of the top 12 independent predictors of thirty day mortality, seven were postoperative (cardiac arrest, failure to wean, systemic sepsis, stroke, renal failure, myocardial infarction and renal insufficiency). Furthermore, complications such as pneumonia, wound infection and pulmonary embolism, even after apparent recovery still result in a shortened lifespan.

In the opinion of the Advisors the complications that were noted affected outcome in 56/213 (26%) of cases.

Given the high incidence of postoperative complications and the impact this has on patient outcome there is an urgent need to improve care pathways so that avoidable postoperative complications are minimised.

Having identified problems with pre and peri-operative fluid therapy, the Advisors thought that there was inadequate record of postoperative fluid balance in 234/755 (30%) of patients. Goal directed therapy pre-, peri- and postoperatively has been shown to improve outcome but not reduce mortality. Cardiac surgery had addressed goal directed therapy in the postoperative period[10]. The Advisors have highlighted the need for a greater attention to accurate and appropriate fluid therapy in the entire operative period.

The Advisors considered the postoperative care to be graded as shown in Table 4.74. In 95% of the peer reviewed patients the Advisors considered the postoperative care to be good and adequate. In 5% they considered the care to be poor or unacceptable.

Table 4.74 Standard of postoperative care received

Standard of care	Number of patients	%
Good	263	46.8
Adequate	273	48.6
Poor	24	4.3
Unacceptable	2	<1
Subtotal	**562**	
Insufficient data to assign grade	44	
Unanswered	223	
Total	**829**	

When looking at the Advisors opinion of different stages of care Table 4.75 is produced. In the pre-operative period care was judged as poor or unacceptable in 10% of elective patients and 12% of non-elective patients. In the operative period these less acceptable levels of care fell to 2% and then in the postoperative period care was poor or unacceptable in 5% of patients. When taking an overall view of the care pathway of high risk patients the most improvement appears to be needed outside the operating theatre in the pre and postoperative period.

Table 4.75 Standard of care at different stages

Care	Pre-operative (Elective)	%	Pre-operative (Non-elective)	%	Intra-operative	%	Postoperative	%
Good	165	37.6	86	38.7	380	53.4	263	46.8
Adequate	217	49.4	114	51.4	313	44.0	273	48.6
Poor	51	11.6	20	9.0	16	2.3	24	4.3
Unacceptable	6	1.4	2	<1	2	<1	2	<1
Subtotal	**439**		**222**		**711**		**562**	
Unable to assign grade	111		43		118		247	
Total	**550**		**265**		**829**		**829**	

Key Findings - Peer review data

Overall the care of patients was good in only 48% of high risk patients.

The review of the high risk cases by the NCEPOD Advisors uncovered a lack of consensus as to what constitutes high peri-operative risk.

67% of these high risk patients were overweight.

In only 37/496 patients was any mention of mortality made on the consent forms.

Only 6.1% of patients had a documented plan to improve their pre-operative nutritional status.

For those patients in the non-elective group 95.7% had a timely initial assessment and 98.8% had a documented management plan.

98% of high risk elective patients received appropriately timed surgery. In comparison 80% of non-elective patients received timely surgery. One in five non-elective high risk patients were delayed going to theatre.

The 30 day mortality in those patients in whom the Advisors considered there to have been inadequate pre-operative fluid management was 20.5% compared to 4.7% mortality in those with adequate pre-operative fluid therapy. This reinforces previous evidence outlining the beneficial effects on outcome of optimisation of fluid status prior to surgery.

Patients who suffered intra-operative complications had a 30 day mortality of 13.2% compared to 5.7% in those without.

Cardiac output monitoring was rarely used in high risk patients.

Inadequate intra-operative monitoring was associated with a three fold increase in mortality.

In only 19/550 elective patients was there any record of entrance into any form of enhanced recovery programme.

For those high risk patients not discharged to a higher care level area 360/489 (74%) had records of being in an early warning scoring system or track and trigger system for the detection of a deterioration in their physiological status.

8.3% of high risk patients who should have gone to a higher care level area postoperatively did not do so.

The Advisors considered that postoperative complications had affected outcome in 56/213 (26%) of cases.

Recommendations

All elective high risk patients should be seen and fully investigated in pre-assessment clinics. Arrangements should be in place to ensure more urgent surgical patients have the same robust work up. (Clinical Directors and Consultants)

Greater assessment of nutritional status and its correction should be employed in high risk patients. (Consultants)

High risk patients should have fluid optimisation in a higher care level area pre-operatively, if it is to be adequate and contribute to better outcomes. (Consultants)

The adoption of enhanced recovery pathways for high risk elective patients should be promoted. (Clinical Directors)

Given the high incidence of postoperative complications demonstrated in the review of high risk patients, and the impact this has on outcome there is an urgent need to address postoperative care; this supports the prospective data.* (Clinical Directors)

*Recommendation from page 46
The postoperative care of the high risk surgical patient needs to be improved. Each Trust must make provision for sufficient critical care beds or pathways of care to provide appropriate support in the postoperative period. (Medical Directors)

Summary

This study is very important for NCEPOD for two main reasons. Firstly it is a change to the usual study method. Secondly it has revealed that there are many remediable factors in the peri-operative care pathway of high risk surgical patients.

This is the first time that NCEPOD has collected data prospectively. Data was collected on all eligible surgical procedures over a one week period. This allowed us to gather a large data set and fully describe the characteristics of this group of patients and pathways of current care. This provided us with denominator data and ensured that our findings were not skewed by a biased sample group. This has long been a criticism of NCEPOD – when we focus on a group with adverse outcomes (e.g. death) it is unsurprising that many remediable factors are found but it is often questioned if these findings can be extrapolated to the whole population. To complement this robust prospective dataset we looked deeper into the care of a group of high risk patients. This relied on peer review of medical notes and other documentation by a group of Advisors. The peer review process allowed opinion to be formed about aspects of patient care and this qualitative assessment supports and enriches the quantitative data from the prospective dataset.

The two sections of the study provide a complete story of the care of high risk surgical patients and highlight the areas of concern.

There are difficulties in identifying high risk patients. However somewhere between 1 in 10 and 1 in 20 of surgical cases should be considered high risk. This is a very significant volume of patients.

There are deficiencies in pre-operative assessment Management of patients prior to surgery was a concern, particularly in non-elective patients, and fluid management was a common problem.

- Intra-operative monitoring for high risk patients rarely included cardiac output monitoring despite the evidence base.
- Critical care was the post operative location for 1 in 5 high risk patients. Most high risk patients return to ward care.
- The high risk group 30 day mortality was almost 7% and this encompassed three quarters of the postoperative deaths.
- Advisors' opinion was that care was good in less than half the cases.

These points highlight that there are major deficiencies in how high risk surgical patients are cared for. As a result, the high risk surgical group has poor outcomes (death and morbidity) and the resultant health care resource utilisation is significant. This study provides some recommendations to remedy this situation and supports the conclusions of the report published by the Royal College of Surgeons of England on the higher risk general surgical patent[37]. Improvement will require both a change in thinking from health professionals about the need of this group and support from health service managers to provide the resources to do so. The returns could be significant – less postoperative death and morbidity, quicker return to health and independent living, more efficient care and less cost to the NHS.

References

1. Niskanen MM, Takala JA: Use of resources and post-operative outcome. *Eur J Surg* 2001, 167:643-649

2. Pearse RM, Harrison DA and James P et al. Identification and characterisation of the high-risk surgical population in the United Kingdom. *Crit Care.* 2006; 10(3):R81. Epub 2006 Jun 2

3. Bennett-Guerrero E et al. Comparison of P-POSSUM risk-adjusted mortality rates after surgery between patients in the United States of America and the United Kingdom. *British Journal of Surgery* 2003; 90: 1593-1598

4. Feachem RG et al. Getting more for their dollar: a comparison of the NHS with California's Kaiser Permanente. *British Medical Journal* 2002; 324: 135-141

5. Shoemaker WC, Appel PL, Bland R. Use of physiologic monitoring to predict outcome and to assist in clinical decisions in critically ill postoperative patients. *Am J Surg* 1983, 146:43-50

6. Boyd O, Grounds RM, Bennett ED. A randomized clinical trial of the effect of deliberate peri-operative increase of oxygen delivery on mortality in high-risk surgical patients. *JAMA* 1993, 270:2699-2707

7. Wilson J, Woods I, Fawcett J, Whall R, Dibb W, Morris C, McManus E. Reducing the risk of major elective surgery: randomised controlled trial of pre-operative optimisation of oxygen delivery. BMJ 1999, 318:1099-1103

8. Lobo SM, Salgado PF and Castillo VG et al. Effects of maximising oxygen delivery on morbidity and mortality in high-risk surgical patients. *Crit Care Med* 2000, 10:3396-3404

9. Sinclair S, James S, Singer M. Intraoperative intravascular volume optimisation and length of hospital stay after repair of proximal femoral fracture: randomised controlled trial. *BMJ* 1997, 315:909-912

10. Pearse R, Dawson D and Fawcett J et al. Early goal-directed therapy after major surgery reduces complications and duration of hospital stay. A randomised, controlled trial [ISRCTN38797445]. *Crit Care* 2005, 9:R687- R693

11. Grocott MPW, Hamilton MA and Bennett ED et al. Perioperative increase in global blood flow to explicit defined goals and outcomes following surgery (Cochrane Protocol). Cochrane Database Syst Rev 2006:Issue 2

12. Kuper M, Gold SJ and Callow C et al. Intraoperative fluid management guided by oesophageal Doppler monitoring. *BMJ* 2011;342:d3016 doi: 10.1136/bmj. d3016

13. National institute for Health and Clinical Excellence. Medical Technology Guidance 3. CardioQ-ODM (oesophageal Doppler monitor) 2011http://www. nice.org.uk/guidance/MTG3

14. Lee TH, Marcantonio ER, Mangione CM, et al. Derivation and prospective validation of a simple index for prediction of cardiac risk of major noncardiac surgery. Circulation 1999;100:1043-1049

15. National Confidential Enquiry into Perioperative Death. *Who Operates When* 1997. London

16. National Confidential Enquiry into Perioperative Death. *Who Operates When II* 2003. London

17. National Confidential Enquiry into Patient Outcome and Death. *Caring to the End* 2009. London

18. National Institute for Health and Clinical Excellence. Clinical Guideline 50. Acutely ill patients in hospital. 2007. http://guidance.nice.org.uk/CG50

19. National Confidential Enquiry into Patient Outcome and Death. *An Acute Problem* 2005. London

20 British Association of Parenteral and Enteral Nutrition. Malnutrition Universal Screening Tool (MUST) www.bapen.org.uk/pdfs/must/must_full.pdf

21. National Institute for Health and Clinical Excellence. Clinical Guideline 65. Perioperative hypothermia (inadvertent). 2007. http://guidance.nice.org.uk/CG65

22. National Confidential Enquiry into Patient Outcome of Death. Classification of intervention. www.ncepod.org.uk/NCEPODClassification.pdf

23. Association of Anaesthetists of Great Britain and Ireland. Recommendations for standards of monitoring during anaesthesia and recovery 4th edition. 2007 http://www.aagbi.org/sites/default/files/standardsofmonitoring07.pdf

24. Statistics on obesity, physical activity and diet: England, 2010 The Health and social care information centre. NHS 2010

25. Pre-operative Assessment and patient preparation. The role of the anaesthetist. AAGB&I 2010

26. Rai J, Gill SS, Kumar BR. The influence of pre-operative nutritional status in wound healing after replacement arthroplasty. *Orthopedics* 2002; 25: 417-2

27. Figueiredo F, Dickson ER and Pasha T et al. Impact of nutritional status on outcomes after liver transplantation. *Transplantation* 2000; 70: 1347-52

28. Heys SD, Gardner E. Nutrients and the surgical patient: current and potential therapeutic applications to clinical practice. *J R Coll Surg Edinb* 1999; 44: 283-93

29. There are NICE guidelines indicating the need to identify and correct preoperative nutritional impairment

30. The General Medical Council requires that doctors must have effective discussions with patients about risk

31. National Confidential Enquiry into Perioperative Deaths. The Report of the *National Confidential Enquiry into Perioperative Deaths*. 2002 London

32. Wilson J, Woods I and Fawcett J et al. Reducing the risk of major elective surgery: randomised controlled trial of preoperative optimization of oxygen delivery BMJ. 1999: 318

33. British Consensus Guidelines on Intravenous Fluid Therapy for Adult Surgical Patients (GIFTASUP). http://www.bapen.org.uk/pdfs/bapen-pubs/giftasup.pdf

34. *The Lancet, Volume 371*, Issue 9625, Page 1661, 17 May 2008

35. National Confidential Enquiry into Patient Outcome and Death. *Adding Insult to Injury* 2009. London

36. Khuri SF, Henderson WG and DePalma RG et al. Participants in the VA National Surgical Quality Improvement Program. Determinants of long-term survival after major surgery and the adverse effect of postoperative complications. *Ann Surg.* 2005 Sep;242(3):326-41

37. The Royal College of Surgeons of England and Department of Health. The higher risk general surgical patient: Towards improved care for a forgotten group. 2011 London

Appendix 1

Glossary

Anastomosis	An anastomosis is a surgical connection between two structures. For example, when part of an intestine is surgically removed, the two remaining ends are sewn or stapled together (anastomosed), and the procedure is referred to as an intestinal anastomosis.
Arterial catheter	A thin, hollow tube placed inside an artery.
ASA grade	The American Society of Anesthesiologists (ASA) physical status classification system grades the fitness of patients before surgery. Where ASA1 is a healthy patient and ASA5 where the patient won't survive without an operation.
Body Mass Index (BMI)	An individual's body weight divided by the square of his or her height to estimate the amount of body fat.
Cardiac output monitoring	A measurement of the volume of blood being pumped by the heart.
Cardiopulmonary exercise testing (CPEX)	A means of assessing heart and lung function and how they work together during exercise.
Central venous catheter	A thin, hollow tube placed inside a major vein.
CEPOD theatre	A dedicated, staffed emergency operating theatre available 24 hours/day, 7 days/week.
Comorbidities	Another disease or disorder which may affect the primary disease.
Critical care	Intensive care/high dependency care.
Cerebrovascular accident (CVA)	A stroke lasting more than 24 hours
Early warning scores	Processes to alert health care professionals that a patient's condition is worsening.
GMC	General Medical Council
Hypothermia	When the core body temperature drops below the required level to function.
Hypovolaemia	A state of decreased blood volume.
NHS	National Health Service
NICE	National Institute for Health and Clinical Excellence
NSAIDs	Non-steroidal anti-inflammatory drugs
PACU	Post anaesthetic care unit
Risk stratification (in the context of this report)	A means of assessing a patient's risk of morbidity or mortality peri-operatively
Transient ischaemic attack (TIA)	A small stroke lasting less than 24 hours
Track and trigger	Thresholds over which a patient's deterioration will be noted and action taken.
Triage	The process of determining the priority of patients' treatments based on the severity of their condition.
Urgency of surgery	NCEPOD classification defined as elective, emergency, urgent and expedited. Details can be found at www.ncepod.org.uk.
Vaso-active drugs	Drugs that dilate or restrict arteries or veins to affect things such as blood pressure.
Ventilatory support	A means of supporting a patient's breathing.

Appendix 2

Six month outcome data

This study aimed to link the prospective dataset to data from the Office for National Statistics (ONS) for England and Wales to provide 6 month outcome data for all patients. Cases were linked using NHS number in the first instance and if NHS number was not available then matching was undertaken using name and date of birth. Data were also collected from each hospital relating to the 30 mortality (presented earlier in the report) which could be used for cross-checking against ONS.

For cases with NHS numbers matching was straightforward and the table below shows the 30 day and 6 month outcome for these cases classified by risk.

However, review of the cases matched to ONS by fields other than NHS highlighted considerable difficulties in linking the databases and reconciling individual patients. Matching on name and date of birth resulted in some cases with up to 50 matches from ONS. Without greater detail it was impossible to identify which, if any, was the matching record.

Outcome	Low risk			High risk		
	Alive	Deceased	% mortality	Alive	Deceased	% mortality
30 days	9155	29	0.3	2397	102	4.1
6 months	9071	113	1.2	2254	245	9.8

Furthermore, there were a number of patients who had been reported as having died within 30 days of surgery that were not included in the ONS dataset of deaths. This may be due to delays in coding/reporting to ONS or the fact that in some cases outcome was reported to NCEPOD but not enough patient details to match with ONS.

Whilst the sample size in the table above is large and likely to be somewhat representative, it does not reflect the total patient group included in this report and as such could not be included in the full analysis. It is provided here for information.

Appendix 3

Corporate structure and role of NCEPOD

The National Confidential Enquiry into Patient Outcome and Death (NCEPOD) is an independent body to which a corporate commitment has been made by the Medical and Surgical Colleges, Associations and Faculties related to its area of activity. Each of these bodies nominates members on to NCEPOD's Steering Group.

The role of NCEPOD

The role of NCEPOD is to describe the gap between the care that should be delivered and what actually happens on the ground. In some ways it is a glorious anachronism: an exercise by the professions themselves to criticise the care that they deliver in the cause of improving the quality of the Service.

The process is simple but effective. We begin with an idea. Subjects can be suggested by anyone, but most come from the professional associations. It is measure of how deeply the medical profession are committed to the improvement of their service that they should be voluble and enthusiastic about having the care that they deliver assessed and criticised by their peers.

To run the study robustly the staff and Clinical Co-ordinators, together with an Expert Group work up the study design so as to get the raw material that they think they will need to explore the quality of care. They identify a given group of cases and design the study and the questionnaires.

The NCEPOD Local Reporters – our precious eyes and ears in every Trust - are then asked to identify all the cases falling within that cohort. We then send all the Consultants responsible for those cases a questionnaire and elicit the key data that we need. We also ask the Trusts for copies of the notes.

Our staff then go through the notes laboriously anonymising them so that the Advisors and Authors cannot identify the patient, the hospital or the staff involved. Inevitably from time to time a perspicacious Advisor will recognise a colleague's handwriting, or even a case from a hospital they have worked at: they are trusted to quietly replace it on the pile and draw another.

The Advisors are specialists in the areas of the study but they are emphatically not members of the expert group and play no part in the design of the study. They may have no prior connection with NCEPOD but wish to contribute to the over-riding aim of improving care in their specialty. They are trained, being put through dummy runs together with our Co-ordinators, so as to develop the necessary consistency of approach. Their assessment of the cases is done in our premises, in group meetings. Most cases will only be read by one Advisor who fills in a questionnaire, but they work together and discuss striking features as they come across them, so that the finished report and the vignettes do not represent idiosyncratic opinions. As you can see from our Acknowledgements they are a multidisciplinary group of distinguished professionals and the final report is compiled by the Co-ordinators and our staff from the material and the judgements made by them, for which we are deeply grateful.

Steering Group as at 9th December 2011

Dr I Wilson	Association of Anaesthetists of Great Britain and Ireland
Mr F Smith	Association of Surgeons of Great Britain & Ireland
Mr J Wardrope	College of Emergency Medicine
Dr S Bridgman	Faculty of Public Health Medicine
Professor R Mahajan	Royal College of Anaesthetists
Dr A Batchelor	Royal College of Anaesthetists
Dr B Ellis	Royal College of General Practitioners
Ms M McElligott	Royal College of Nursing
Dr E Morris	Royal College of Obstetricians and Gynaecologists
Mrs M Wishart	Royal College of Ophthalmologists
Dr I Doughty	Royal College of Paediatrics and Child Health
Dr R Dowdle	Royal College of Physicians
Professor T Hendra	Royal College of Physicians
Dr S McPherson	Royal College of Radiologists
Mr R Lamont	Royal College of Surgeons of England
Mr M Bircher	Royal College of Surgeons of England
Mr D Mitchell	Faculty of Dental Surgery, Royal College of Surgeons of England
Dr M Osborn	Royal College of Pathologists
Ms S Panizzo	Patient Representative
Mrs M Wang	Patient Representative

Observers

Mrs J Mooney	Healthcare Quality Improvement Partnership
Dr R Hunter	Coroners' Society of England and Wales
Dr N Pace	Scottish Audit of Surgical Mortality
Professor P Littlejohns	National Institute for Health and Clinical Excellence

NCEPOD is a company, limited by guarantee (Company number: 3019382) and a registered charity (Charity number: 1075588), managed by Trustees.

Trustees

Mr Bertie Leigh - Chairman
Dr D Justins - Honorary Treasurer
Professor M Britton
Professor J H Shepherd
Professor L Regan
Professor R Endacott

Company Secretary - Dr M Mason

Clinical Co-ordinators

The Steering Group appoint a Lead Clinical Co-ordinator for a defined tenure. In addition there are seven Clinical Co-ordinators who work on each study. All Co-ordinators are engaged in active academic/clinical practice (in the NHS) during their term of office.

Lead Clinical Co-ordinator	Dr G Findlay (Intensive Care)
Clinical Co-ordinators	Dr D G Mason (Anaesthesia)
	Dr K Wilkinson (Anaesthesia)
	Dr A P L Goodwin (Anaesthesia)
	Professor S B Lucas (Pathology)
	Mr I C Martin (Surgery)
	Professor M J Gough (Surgery)

Supporting organisations

The organisations that provided funding to cover the cost
of this study:
National Patient Safety Agency on behalf of the
Department of Health in England and the Welsh Assembly
Government
Department of Health, Social Services and Public Safety
(Northern Ireland)
Aspen Healthcare Ltd
BMI Healthcare
BUPA Cromwell
Classic Hospitals
East Kent Medical Services Ltd
Fairfield Independent Hospital
HCA International
Hospital of St John and St Elizabeth
Isle of Man Health and Social Security Department
King Edward VII's Hospital Sister Agnes
New Victoria Hospital
Nuffield Health
Ramsay Health Care UK
Spire Health Care
St Anthony's Hospital
St Joseph's Hospital
States of Guernsey Board of Health
States of Jersey, Health and Social Services
The Horder Centre
The Hospital Management Trust
The London Clinic
Ulster Independent Clinic

Appendix 4

Participation

Trust	Number of sites	Number of prospective forms	Spreadsheets received	Number of cases included for peer review	Number of sets of case notes returned	Organisational questionnaires received
Abertawe Bro Morgannwg University Health Board	4	326	4	20	19	4
Aintree Hospitals NHS Foundation Trust	1	115	1	0	0	1
Airedale NHS Trust	1	44	1	6	6	1
Aneurin Bevan Local Health Board	4	210	4	13	13	4
Ashford & St Peter's Hospital NHS Trust	2	32	2	4	4	2
Aspen Healthcare	2	30	2	0	0	2
Barking, Havering & Redbridge University Hospitals NHS Trust	2	100	2	11	11	2
Barnet and Chase Farm Hospitals NHS Trust	2	163	2	11	9	2
Barnsley Hospital NHS Foundation Trust	1	71	1	2	2	1
Barts and The London NHS Trust	3	113	3	13	7	3
Basildon & Thurrock University Hospitals NHS FoundationTrust	1	37	1	6	5	1
Basingstoke & North Hampshire Hospitals NHS Foundation Trust	1	123	1	6	6	1
Bedford Hospital NHS Trust	1	68	1	6	6	1
Belfast Health and Social Care Trust	4	310	4	24	19	4
Benenden Hospital	1	35	1	6	6	1
Betsi Cadwaladr University Local Health Board	5	269	3	13	0	5
Birmingham Women's Healthcare NHS Trust	1	25	1	6	6	1
Blackpool, Fylde and Wyre Hospitals NHS Foundation Trust	1	87	1	6	6	1
BMI Healthcare	32	413	22	21	16	32
Bradford Teaching Hospitals NHS Foundation Trust	1	153	1	6	6	1
Brighton and Sussex University Hospitals NHS Trust	2	130	2	9	9	2
Buckinghamshire Healthcare NHS Trust	2	89	2	11	11	2
BUPA Cromwell Hospital	1	4	1	3	2	1
Burton Hospitals NHS Foundation Trust	1	76	1	2	2	1
Calderdale & Huddersfield NHS Foundation Trust	2	201	2	13	13	2
Cambridge University Hospitals NHS Foundation Trust	1	207	1	6	4	1
Cardiff and Vale University Health Board	2	90	2	9	9	2
Care UK	4	101	1	1	1	4
Central Manchester University Hospitals NHS Foundation Trust	3	85	3	0	0	3
Chelsea & Westminster Healthcare NHS Trust	1	32	1	2	0	1
City Hospitals Sunderland NHS Foundation Trust	2	143	2	7	7	2
Colchester Hospital University NHS Foundation Trust	1	106	1	6	6	1
Countess of Chester Hospital NHS Foundation Trust	1	103	1	6	6	1
County Durham and Darlington NHS Foundation Trust	3	118	3	9	9	3
Croydon Health Services NHS Trust	1	34	1	5	5	1
Cwm Taf Local Health Board	2	154	2	12	12	2

Trust	Number of sites	Number of prospective forms	Spreadsheets received	Number of cases included for peer review	Number of sets of case notes returned	Organisational questionnaires received
Dartford & Gravesham NHS Trust	1	60	0	0	0	1
Derby Hospitals NHS Foundation Trust	1	82	1	5	5	1
Doncaster and Bassetlaw Hospitals NHS Foundation Trust	3	168	3	8	8	3
Dorset County Hospital NHS Foundation Trust	1	38	1	6	6	1
Dorset Primary Care Trust	1	0	1	0	0	1
Ealing Hospital NHS Trust	1	19	0	0	0	1
East & North Hertfordshire NHS Trust	2	139	2	7	7	2
East Kent Hospitals University NHS Foundation Trust	3	207	3	18	5	3
East Kent Medical Services	1	0	0	0	0	1
East Lancashire Hospitals NHS Trust	2	89	2	8	7	2
East Sussex Healthcare NHS Trust	2	74	2	8	8	2
Epsom and St Helier University Hospitals NHS Trust	3	26	1	1	1	3
Fairfield Independent Hospital	1	11	1	0	0	1
Frimley Park Hospitals NHS Trust	1	114	1	2	2	1
Gateshead Health NHS Foundation Trust	1	36	1	6	6	1
George Eliot Hospital NHS Trust	1	5	1	0	0	1
Gloucestershire Hospitals NHS Foundation Trust	2	85	2	11	3	2
Great Western Hospitals NHS Foundation Trust	1	54	1	3	3	1
Guy's & St Thomas' NHS Foundation Trust	2	76	0	0	0	2
Harrogate and District NHS Foundation Trust	1	0	1	0	0	1
HCA International	1	49	1	3	3	1
Heart of England NHS Foundation Trust	3	28	3	5	0	3
Heatherwood & Wexham Park Hospitals NHS Foundation Trust	2	0	2	0	0	2
Hillingdon Hospital NHS Trust	2	69	2	9	9	2
Hinchingbrooke Health Care NHS Trust	1	38	1	6	0	1
Homerton University Hospital NHS Foundation Trust	1	43	1	6	5	1
Hospital of St John and St Elizabeth	1	39	0	0	0	1
Hull and East Yorkshire Hospitals NHS Trust	3	197	2	12	10	3
Hywel Dda Local Health Board	4	180	4	21	22	4
Imperial College Healthcare NHS Trust	4	189	3	18	18	4
Ipswich Hospital NHS Trust	1	126	1	6	6	1
Isle of Wight NHS Primary Care Trust	1	45	0	0	0	1
James Paget Healthcare NHS Trust	1	80	1	6	6	1
King Edward VII's Hospital Sister Agnes	1	32	1	1	1	1
King's College Hospital NHS Foundation Trust	1	0	1	0	0	1
Kingston Hospital NHS Trust	1	81	1	6	6	1
Lancashire Teaching Hospitals NHS Foundation Trust	2	88	2	7	7	2
Leeds Teaching Hospitals NHS Trust (The)	3	395	3	20	15	3
Lewisham Hospital NHS Trust	1	31	1	6	6	1

Participation *(continued)*

Trust	Number of sites	Number of prospective forms	Spreadsheets received	Number of cases included for peer review	Number of sets of case notes returned	Organisational questionnaires received
Liverpool Heart and Chest Hospital NHS Trust	1	25	1	6	6	1
Liverpool Women's NHS Foundation Trust	1	43	0	0	0	1
London Clinic	1	0	1	0	0	1
Luton and Dunstable Hospital NHS Foundation Trust	1	68	1	6	5	1
Maidstone and Tunbridge Wells NHS Trust	3	107	3	13	8	3
Mid Cheshire Hospitals NHS Foundation Trust	1	82	1	6	6	1
Mid Staffordshire NHS Foundation Trust	2	43	2	1	1	2
Mid Yorkshire Hospitals NHS Trust	3	178	3	17	17	3
Mid-Essex Hospital Services NHS Trust	2	217	2	8	8	2
Milton Keynes Hospital NHS Foundation Trust	1	90	1	6	2	1
New Victoria Hospital	1	17	1	1	1	1
Newcastle upon Tyne Hospitals NHS Foundation Trust	3	232	3	11	10	3
Newham University Hospital NHS Trust	1	73	0	0	0	1
NHS Surrey	1	0	1	0	0	1
NHS West Sussex	2	0	2	0	0	2
Norfolk & Norwich University Hospital NHS Trust	1	287	1	6	0	1
North Bristol NHS Trust	2	147	2	18	17	2
North Middlesex University Hospital NHS Trust	1	53	1	6	0	1
North Tees and Hartlepool NHS Foundation Trust	2	78	2	12	11	2
North West London Hospitals NHS Trust	2	91	2	13	13	2
Northampton General Hospital NHS Trust	1	107	1	6	6	1
Northern Devon Healthcare NHS Trust	1	64	1	4	4	1
Northern Lincolnshire & Goole Hospitals NHS Foundation Trust	2	138	2	12	12	2
Northumbria Healthcare NHS Foundation Trust	3	98	3	10	10	3
Nottingham University Hospitals NHS Trust	2	279	2	12	12	2
Nuffield Health	13	209	11	7	7	13
Oxford Radcliffe Hospital NHS Trust	5	118	5	17	16	5
Papworth Hospital NHS Foundation Trust	1	11	1	5	5	1
Pennine Acute Hospitals NHS Trust (The)	4	223	4	24	24	4
Peterborough & Stamford Hospitals NHS Foundation Trust	2	132	2	12	12	2
Plymouth Hospitals NHS Trust	1	181	0	0	0	1
Poole Hospital NHS Foundation Trust	1	92	1	6	3	1
Portsmouth Hospitals NHS Trust	1	231	1	6	6	1
Princess Alexandra Hospital NHS Trust	1	74	1	6	6	1
Queen Victoria Hospital NHS Foundation Trust	1	87	1	0	0	1
Robert Jones and Agnes Hunt Orthopaedic Hospital NHS Foundation Trust	1	94	1	6	6	1
Royal Berkshire NHS Foundation Trust	1	114	1	6	6	1
Royal Bolton Hospital NHS Foundation Trust	1	103	1	6	7	1

Trust	Number of sites	Number of prospective forms	Spreadsheets received	Number of cases included for peer review	Number of sets of case notes returned	Organisational questionnaires received
Royal Bournemouth and Christchurch Hospitals NHS Trust	1	124	1	6	6	1
Royal Brompton and Harefield NHS Trust	1	22	0	0	0	1
Royal Cornwall Hospitals NHS Trust	3	143	3	6	6	3
Royal Devon and Exeter NHS Foundation Trust	1	199	1	6	6	1
Royal Free Hampstead NHS Trust	2	151	1	6	6	2
Royal Liverpool & Broadgreen University Hospitals NHS Trust	1	207	1	6	6	1
Royal Marsden NHS Foundation Trust (The)	2	66	2	5	5	2
Royal National Orthopaedic Hospital NHS Trust	1	90	1	6	6	1
Royal Surrey County Hospital NHS Trust	1	103	1	6	6	1
Royal United Hospital Bath NHS Trust	1	112	1	6	6	1
Royal Wolverhampton Hospitals NHS Trust (The)	1	102	1	6	0	1
Salford Royal Hospitals NHS Foundation Trust	1	95	1	5	5	1
Salisbury NHS FoundationTrust	1	142	1	6	6	1
Sandwell and West Birmingham Hospitals NHS Trust	2	137	2	2	2	2
Scarborough and North East Yorkshire Health Care NHS Trust	1	19	0	0	0	1
Sheffield Teaching Hospitals NHS Foundation Trust	2	266	2	12	9	2
Sherwood Forest Hospitals NHS Foundation Trust	2	96	2	6	6	2
Shrewsbury and Telford Hospitals NHS Trust	2	131	2	10	10	2
South Devon Healthcare NHS Foundation Trust	1	86	1	6	6	1
South Eastern Health & Social Care Trust	2	43	2	0	0	2
South London Healthcare NHS Trust	3	184	3	11	11	3
South Tees Hospitals NHS Foundation Trust	2	167	2	7	7	2
South Tyneside NHS Foundation Trust	1	25	1	5	4	1
South Warwickshire NHS Foundation Trust	1	71	1	8	8	1
Southampton University Hospitals NHS Trust	2	190	2	7	5	2
Southern Health & Social Care Trust	2	27	2	0	0	2
Southern Healthcare NHS Foundation Trust	1	3	1	0	0	1
Southport and Ormskirk Hospitals NHS Trust	2	72	2	6	6	2
Spire Healthcare	29	616	24	39	34	29
St Anthony's Hospital	1	53	1	5	5	1
St George's Healthcare NHS Trust	1	216	1	6	6	1
St Helens and Knowsley Teaching Hospitals NHS Trust	1	114	1	4	4	1
Stockport NHS Foundation Trust	1	0	1	0	0	1
Surrey & Sussex Healthcare NHS Trust	1	124	1	6	6	1
Taunton & Somerset NHS Foundation Trust	1	163	1	9	9	1
The Christie NHS Foundation Trust	1	32	1	3	3	1
The Dudley Group of Hospitals	1	123	1	8	8	1
The Horder Centre	1	50	1	0	0	1

Participation *(continued)*

Trust	Number of sites	Number of prospective forms	Spreadsheets received	Number of cases included for peer review	Number of sets of case notes returned	Organisational questionnaires received
The Hospital Management Trust	2	6	1	0	0	2
The Queen Elizabeth Hospital King's Lynn NHS Trust	1	87	0	0	0	1
The Rotherham NHS Foundation Trust	1	83	1	7	7	1
Trafford Healthcare NHS Trust	1	19	1	4	4	1
UK Specialist Hospitals Ltd	1	15	1	0	0	1
United Lincolnshire Hospitals NHS Trust	4	194	4	16	16	4
Univ. Hospital of South Manchester NHS Foundation Trust	1	132	1	6	6	1
University College London Hospitals NHS Foundation Trust	3	157	3	8	8	3
University Hospital Birmingham NHS Foundation Trust	2	126	2	12	12	2
University Hospital of North Staffordshire NHS Trust	2	119	2	6	6	2
University Hospitals Coventry and Warwickshire NHS Trust	2	232	2	7	7	2
University Hospitals of Bristol NHS Foundation Trust	4	145	3	6	6	4
University Hospitals of Leicester NHS Trust	3	258	3	15	15	3
University Hospitals of Morecambe Bay NHS Trust	3	139	3	9	9	3
West Hertfordshire Hospitals NHS Trust	1	76	0	0	0	1
West Middlesex University Hospital NHS Trust	1	20	1	4	4	1
West Suffolk Hospitals NHS Trust	1	116	1	0	0	1
Western Health & Social Care Trust	2	102	2	10	10	2
Western Sussex Hospitals NHS Trust	3	218	3	14	6	3
Weston Area Health Trust	1	52	1	6	6	1
Whipps Cross University Hospital NHS Trust	1	96	1	6	6	1
Whittington Health	1	84	1	5	5	1
Wirral University Teaching Hospital NHS Foundation Trust	2	118	1	6	0	2
Wrightington, Wigan & Leigh NHS Foundation Trust	2	69	2	11	11	2
Wye Valley NHS Trust	1	51	1	6	6	1
Yeovil District Hospital NHS Foundation Trust	1	78	1	6	6	1
York Hospitals NHS Foundation Trust	1	101	1	6	6	1

The above table lists all the Trusts that contributed data
to the study. Where the number of cases included for
peer review is 0, either no high risk cases were identified
by the anaesthetists completing the prospective forms
or the spreadsheet data did not match the prospective
form data.